What Others are Saying about Dig Deep

"I am sure of this — If you hope to get most boys to read, the book had better be interesting. I believe *Dig Deep* will "hook" boys with its captivating stories, activities, and projects. Rebecca has made this study fun, while at the same time unashamedly challenging boys to sincerely and faithfully walk with Christ."
—Rev. Bobby Webb, Minister of Education, Parkway Baptist Church, Goodlettsville, TN

"Rebecca Ingram Powell understands and addresses the questions and struggles of today's youth like no other. Captivating readers with compelling stories and amazing wisdom from Solomon's Proverbs, *Dig Deep* equips young teens to study God's Word and apply it to daily life. I highly recommend this powerful study as an essential tool for a boy's journey into spiritual maturity."
—Ginger Plowman, Author, *Don't Make Me Count to Three!*

"The premise of introducing young boys to the wisdom of God's own wise man, King Solomon, is long overdue in curriculum choices. This well-organized lesson material will keep the student immersed in the wonderful treasures he'll find."
—David Longoria, Principal, Aaron Academy

"Those who read the book of Proverbs learn that the truth is the truth no matter when it was written . . . . Truth that is timeless grounds us. It connects us with the past and guides us into the future. Rebecca Ingram Powell gives our youth what will become timelessly good advice in a format that is exciting and current."
—Stephen S. Sawyer, www.art4god.com

"*Dig Deep* cuts through the mixed messages our young men are receiving everyday and challenges them to be men of honesty, faithfulness, and integrity, providing the opportunity to discover that God has a better plan for their lives!"
—Rev. Barry Davis, Senior Pastor, First Baptist Church, Madison, TN

"As a youth pastor, it was always difficult to find quality books and devotionals for the guys to read. *Dig Deep* mixes the treasure of God's Word with the "cool factor" for today's generation. Boys will read this book! *Dig Deep* will give guys a sense of excitement about their faith as they unearth truths they can use everyday in school, their relationships, and at home. Now, as a homeschool dad, I can't wait for my own sons to read *Dig Deep*. I believe it will challenge them to walk closer with Christ and it will also serve as a discussion starter for our own father/son conversations. I highly recommend *Dig Deep* for your young men."
—Dr. Eddie Poole, Mount Juliet, TN

DIG DEEP

Unearthing the Treasures of Solomon's Proverbs

REBECCA INGRAM POWELL

A Division of WINEPRESS PUBLISHING

©2006 by Rebecca Ingram Powell.
All rights reserved.

Layout design by Sherry Walker.
Printed in the United States of America.

Packaged by Pleasant Word, a division of WinePress Publishing, PO Box 428, Enumclaw, WA 98022. The views expressed or implied in this work do not necessarily reflect those of Pleasant Word, a division of WinePress Publishing. Ultimate design, content, and editorial accuracy of this work are the responsibilities of the author.

No part of this work may be reproduced, stored in a retrieval system, or transmitted in any way by any means — electronic, mechanical, photocopy, recording, or otherwise — without the prior permission of the copyright holder. It is illegal and unethical to reproduce copyrighted material without permission. Contact Rebecca Ingram Powell for additional copies: www.rebeccapowell.com.

Unless otherwise noted all Scriptures are taken from the Holy Bible, New International Version, Copyright © 1973, 1978, 1984 by the International Bible Society. Used by permission of Zondervan Publishing House. The "NIV" and "New International Version" trademarks are registered in the United States Patent and Trademark Office by the International Bible Society.

GOD'S WORD is a copyrighted work of God's Word to the Nations. Quotations are used by permission. Copyright 1995 by God's Word to the Nations. All rights reserved. Scripture quotations marked The Message are taken from THE MESSAGE. Copyright © by Eugene Peterson, 1993, 1994, 1995. Used by permission of NavPress Publishing Group. Scripture quotations marked NLT are taken from the Holy Bible, New Living Translation, copyright © 1996. Used by permission of Tyndale House Publishers, Inc., Wheaton, Illinois 60189. All rights reserved.

ISBN: 1-4141-0680-7
Library of Congress Catalog Card Number: 2006900722

To my sons,
David and Derek

You are my blessing and delight.
I love you.

Sons are a heritage from the Lord,
children a reward from Him.
Like arrows in the hands of a warrior
are sons born in one's youth.
Psalms 127:3,4

Table of Contents

Foreword 11

Introduction 13

Unit One • The Beginning of Wisdom
    Preview   16
    Monday   Beginning Your Day: Not by Accident 17
    Tuesday   Beginning Your Relationships: Choosing Friends 21
    Wednesday Beginning Your Teen Years: Wisdom's Cry 25
    Thursday   Beginning Your Life's Legacy: What Goes Around 28
    Friday   Lab Work: Artifacts and Heartifacts.................................32

Unit Two • Facets of Wisdom
    Preview   33
    Monday   Parental Wisdom: Listening to Love and Experience 34
    Tuesday   Protective Wisdom: His Presence in the Storm 38
    Wednesday Discerning Wisdom: When the Buzzer Goes Off...........41
    Thursday   Life Wisdom: The Walk of the Righteous.......................45
    Friday   Lab Work: Artifacts and Heartifacts.................................49

Unit Three • Wisdom along the Way
    Preview   50
    Monday   In All Your Ways: Acknowledging God 51
    Tuesday   Give It Away: Tithes and Treasures 54
    Wednesday Out-of-the-Ways: Bypassing the Drive-Thru 58
    Thursday   Neighboring Ways: Making a Difference 61
    Friday   Lab Work: Artifacts and Heartifacts.................................65

Unit Four • Wisdom Takes the Gold
    Preview   66
    Monday   No Deposit, No Return: The Cost of the Crown............67
    Tuesday   Practice Makes Perfect: An Unlikely Olympian 71

Wednesday	Cheaters Never Prosper: Wisdom Wins First Place	75
Thursday	It's How You Play the Game: A Gracious Victor	79
Friday	Lab Work: Artifacts and Heartifacts	83

Unit Five • Wisdom Defends His Honor

Preview		84
Monday	Exposing the Enemy: Death Dressed Up	85
Tuesday	Preparing for Battle: Staying Inside the Lines	89
Wednesday	A Word of Warning: Sex Has a Price Tag	92
Thursday	Warning Bell: Sounding the Alarm	97
Friday	Lab Work: Artifacts and Heartifacts	101

Unit Six • Wisdom Stays Out of Trouble

Preview		102
Monday	Mouthy Messes: Before It Gets Cold	103
Tuesday	Active Ants: High Hopes for the Greatest Generation	107
Wednesday	Terrible Troublemakers: 7 UPs God Hates	112
Thursday	A Real Relationship: Show and Tell	115
Friday	Lab Work: Artifacts and Heartifacts	118

Unit Seven • Written on Your Heart

Preview		120
Monday	Wisdom Remains on the Sidewalk: Listen to Your Mummy	121
Tuesday	Wisdom Reveals the Enemy: Taken by Surprise	125
Wednesday	Wisdom Retains His Innocence: He Said...She Said	129
Thursday	Wisdom Rests on a Firm Foundation: Christ, the Cornerstone	133
Friday	Lab Work: Artifacts and Heartifacts	137

Unit Eight • Wisdom's Invitation

Preview		138
Monday	Where: A Busy Intersection	139
Tuesday	When: A Daily Date	143
Wednesday	Who: Someone Like You	147

Thursday	RSVP: The Courtesy of a Reply is Requested	151
Friday	Lab Work: Artifacts and Heartifacts	155

Unit Nine • Wisdom Sets a Table

Preview		156
Monday	The Menu: A Myriad of Choices	157
Tuesday	The House Specialty: A Teachable Spirit	161
Wednesday	The Main Course: Cleaning Your Plate	164
Thursday	The Table Scraps: Leftovers	168
Friday	Lab Work: Artifacts and Heartifacts	172

Appendix A: About Quotables 173

Appendix B: Scripturistics (Scripture Memory Guide) 179

Appendix C: Prayermids (A Perpetual Monthly Prayer Calendar) 184

About the Author 193

End Notes 194

Order Page 196

Foreword

A recent *Newsweek* magazine cover story was titled, "The Boy Crisis." It described a declining trend with males along every phase of schooling in America. Here were some of the more glaring stats:

▲ 44% of undergraduate students on college campuses are male. Thirty years ago that number was 58%.
▲ Boys ages 5 to 12 are 60% more likely than girls to have repeated at least one grade.
▲ Eighth grade girls score 21 points higher than boys on standardized writing tests.
▲ 22% more high school girls are planning to go to college than boys.

These numbers make me sad. As a young man, don't they upset you? Aren't you kind of insulted? They make me ask things like, "Hmmm, are boys really getting dumber, or are girls just getting smarter?" It's a fair question, but truthfully, I don't think either option is true. No one is getting "dumber," and no one is really getting smarter. But clearly, the boys are caring less and less. That can't be denied. These stats are in black and white. They are just numbers but they tell a heartbreaking tale. Something is wrong with the young men and boys of America. They seem to have lost their goals. Their vision. Their purpose.

It's to the point where the kind of young man who has these positive characteristics--clear goals, a focused vision, a definite purpose--is somewhat few and far between. *Rare.* Jesus told us that, "The highway to hell is broad and the gate is wide for the many who choose the easy way. But the gateway to life is small, and the road is narrow, and only a few ever find it."[1]

I encourage all young men (YOU!) to be that rare person in this world. Be that young man of God who is set apart. Special. Different. Holy. Yes, holy! Christ's fiery apostle, Peter, (You know the one: He cut that dude's ear off for messing with Jesus.[2] Yeah, *that* Peter!) He challenged all believers to let themselves "be pulled into a way of life shaped by God's life, a life energetic and blazing with holiness. God said, 'I am holy; you be holy.'"[3]

Many young men today would say that such a command is just too difficult in the world we live in. "There are too any distractions," they might say. Sounds like a cop-out to me.

On the other hand, there is that individual, exceptional guy--the standout-- who reads that verse and takes it very seriously. He understands that God means business when He calls His children to live differently than most of society. Such a young man is on a clear course to great blessing and victory! In a word, that young man is *WISE.*

If you are that young man searching for wisdom or a *how to live as God wants me to live* guide to life, I would always point you to the book of Proverbs, the book of wisdom. Proverbs 1:4 tells us, "These proverbs will make the simple-minded clever." Clever....wow, that more than combats the above discouraging stats about boys. The verse goes on to say, "They will give knowledge and purpose to young people."

I find it very interesting that it specifically indicates how Solomon's proverbs will impact *young* people. As a young person, you are like a sponge. Did you know that? You are influenced at a higher rate than an adult, quickly absorbing life and culture. As an adult, I see the importance of constantly directing you to real wisdom, God's wisdom.

Dig Deep: Unearthing the Treasures of Solomon's Proverbs is a book that will point many young men to the wisdom of God. I applaud Rebecca Ingram Powell for her great work here within these pages. I believe with everything in me that any boy or young man who follows this teaching, truly seeking God's will for his life, will find the blessing and victory reserved only for the rare individual. It's offered to all, but only a few really *get it.*

What about you? Do you want to *get it?* Are you that rare person? I encourage you to know that you can be. With God's strength and wisdom in your life, you can have all the blessings He has for you.

—Clay Crosse, three-time Dove Award-winning recording artist

Introduction

Welcome to a Bible study written just for you. *Dig Deep: Unearthing the Treasures of Solomon's Proverbs* is a nine-week, interactive study of the first nine chapters of the Old Testament book of Proverbs. Incredibly, King Solomon's straightforward instructions to his son concerning sex, friendships, finances, and good character are just as valid today. How can this ancient text apply to a guy your age, living in the 21st Century?

Actually, God's Word has a special quality that makes it different from anything else that has ever been written. In Hebrews 4:12, the apostle Paul explained that the Word of God is living and alive. It's inspired by the Holy Spirit. God uses Scripture to reveal His truth to us, and His truth never changes. So what King Solomon taught his son — about life and about people, about success and about failure, about priorities and about possessions — still makes sense today, thousands of years later.

My desire is for you to grow in God's truth and wisdom as you progress through this study. Please don't hurry through the lessons. Bible study should not be done in haste. Take your time. Eliminate any distractions by retreating to a quiet place. This is the most important part of your day. Don't cheat yourself out of the blessing of giving God your full attention.

Let me share with you the special features of this study.

Dig Site. *Dig Deep: Unearthing the Treasures of Solomon's Proverbs* invites you to be a sort of biblical archaeologist. Each day, your study begins at the *Dig Site*, a brief Bible reading. Every week focuses on one chapter of Proverbs. Each day, you will read a portion of that week's chapter.

Artifacts In Situ. "In Situ" means an object or artifact has been left in its original position as data is gathered. Each lesson contains artifacts within the stories that act as information and history markers from which you can learn. The artifacts will fade away, but the wisdom of God's Word can be found in the "heartifacts" you unearth. You'll list the artifacts and heartifacts at the end of each week on Friday's *Lab Work* page.

Today's Treasure. After you read, take a moment to focus on *Today's Treasure*. Archaeologists sometimes go days and even weeks without finding anything of importance. When it comes to Bible study, however, you will always find something valuable. *Today's Treasure* is simply the core of the day's lesson. Let God use this key verse to open your heart to the truths He has for you.

Data Entry. At the end of each day's lesson, you will find several questions. Answer the questions in complete sentences; take the time you need to formulate your thoughts. And remember, you don't have to share these pages with anyone. You're not being graded on this! These questions are formulated in a way that will provoke you to deeper conversations with God. You're old enough now to be seeking the Lord on your own, and you must have a personal walk with Him to get through your teen years successfully. *Dig Deep: Unearthing the Treasures of Solomon's Proverbs* will help you do that by establishing the habit of a daily quiet time of Bible study and prayer, just you and God.

Quotables. Each lesson concludes with a quote from a remarkable Christian man. Brief biographies of these wise men can be found in Appendix A, along with websites and other resources.

Scripturistics! Scripture memory is vitally important to your Christian life. Every day, take some time to work on this. This is explained fully in Appendix B.

Prayeramids. An important part of this Bible study is in Appendix C, *Prayeramids*. You may pray through these 31 prayers every month. They cover just about everything you can think of! At the end of your Bible study time each day, whatever the date is, pray the prayer that corresponds. For example, if today's date were November 6th, pray the 6th prayer. Tomorrow, pray the 7th prayer. There will be days when the prayer happens to fit exactly with your lesson, but there will be days when it doesn't. Just keep praying! You will be covering yourself with a holy armor as you present these petitions to God every day.

Lab Work. Friday is catch-up day. Use this day to read over your data entries, read back through the entire chapter you've studied, and spend time thinking about what you've learned. List the "artifacts" and "heartifacts" you've uncovered during your study. Meditate on the powerful truths you've found by digging deep.

Extra! Each week has a little something extra you can do to enhance your study. These activities are optional, however, they will give you even more opportunity to unearth the treasures of Proverbs!

My prayer for you, young man, is that you will focus on pursuing God through your teen years. These years are short, but they are bursting with choices. Let's study God's Word together and see just how incredible your teen years can be when you choose the way of Wisdom over the ways of the world.

Preview
Unit One • The Beginning of Wisdom

Monday
Beginning Your Day: Not by Accident

Tuesday
Beginning Your Relationships: Choosing Friends

Wednesday
Beginning Your Teen Years: Wisdom's Cry

Thursday
Beginning Your Life's Legacy: What Goes Around

Friday
Lab Work: Artifacts and Heartifacts

This Week's EXTRA
Watch: "Twice Pardoned: An Ex-Con Talks to Parents & Teens"[4]

| **Monday** | **Unit One • The Beginning of Wisdom** |

Beginning Your Day: Not by Accident

One of the greatest archaeological discoveries of all time happened quite by accident.

In 1947, a young Bedouin shepherd named Jum'a Muhammed was searching among the rocky cliffs of the Qumran Valley for a lost goat. His keen eyes noticed an opening in the rocks, and he wondered if it might be deep enough for the goat to have fallen in. Crouching down on hands and knees, he peered inside. It was too dark to see anything, so Jum'a threw in a couple of pebbles. Listening closely, he heard the pebbles crash into what sounded like pottery. Later that evening, Jum'a brought his two cousins back to investigate.

Together, the three boys squirmed into the opening and wriggled their way down. They found several ancient pottery jars containing musty old scrolls of parchment. These young shepherds didn't think their accidental find was valuable. Rather reluctantly, they gathered the jars, somewhat disappointed with the outcome of their adventure.

Over the next several months, Jum'a's discovery made its way into the hands of some men who recognized its value. They realized those musty bits of parchment were actually scrolls of the ancient texts of the Old Testament. Over the next

Dig Site

Read Proverbs 1:1-7

Artifacts In Situ

- parchment
- pottery

Today's Treasure

The fear of the Lord is the beginning of knowledge, but fools despise wisdom and discipline.
Proverbs 1:7

Unearthing the Treasures of Solomon's Proverbs

ten years, the archaeological search that ensued produced thousands of scroll fragments, from a total of eleven caves.

Known today as the Dead Sea Scrolls, many people recognize their discovery as the most significant archaeological find of the twentieth century. Why? The discovery of the scrolls gave a modern generation confidence that the Word of God had been accurately communicated as it was passed down through the ages. The Old Testament that was inscribed on those scrolls was the same Old Testament that people had been reading for centuries.

Discovering and preserving items from people in past times is what the science of archaeology is all about. It begins with the archaeologist locating the dig site. How does he do that? In one of three ways:

Rescue archaeology. An archaeologist knows that artifacts are in a particular area. The objects must be excavated before they decay or are destroyed, so he embarks on a dig.

Planned archaeology. This type of dig is based on a thorough study of a particular area. The archaeologist researches historical documents and photos to determine exactly where he is going to dig and what he expects to find.

Accidental archaeology. An archaeologist, or even someone like a shepherd boy, stumbles upon a remarkable discovery that proves to be a treasure the whole world finds fascinating — like the Dead Sea Scrolls!

As you begin this study of the first nine chapters of Proverbs, you are unearthing treasures. Rather than artifacts (objects produced by humans for functioning effectively in their civilization), the Bible contains "heartifacts" (words spoken by God for living successfully in the culture). You may have been in church all your life. You may think you know what the Bible is all about. But the wonderful thing about Scripture is there is always something new to discover and learn: about the Lord, about yourself, and about others. For the next nine weeks, you must rescue the heartifacts in Proverbs by digging deeply into God's Word, precept upon precept, line upon line.[5]

King Solomon said the fear of the Lord was the beginning of wisdom. In other words, the first step in learning is bowing down to God.[6] That happens daily, and not by accident. It calls for discipline and determination — character traits a godly young man must strive to cultivate, on purpose. The king wrote the first nine chapters of Proverbs especially for his son. He wanted to teach him about life, relationships, and growing up.

This is a special time in your life. Sure, it's an awkward time. Things are happening to your body and your mind that can make some days seem really weird. But God has a purpose and a plan for your life. Everything that is happening to you is taking you one step closer to manhood. And God can use a man like you! In fact, He can use you right now — right where you are.

Decide on a place and time that you will work on these lessons each day. Guard your study time jealously. Ask your parents and siblings to respect your time alone with God. Ask God to help you be faithful as you commit to establishing this habit of daily devotions.

Data Entry

🖊 Have you ever stumbled upon something valuable? What happened?

_____

_____

_____

🖊 Copy Proverbs 1:7 here in the Bible version you most enjoy using. (If you don't have a favorite, see what versions you have available at home. Use one you can understand.)

_____

_____

_____

✏️ Another word for fear is reverence, which means a feeling of deep awe, respect, and often love. What are some ways you show God your reverence for Him?

_____

_____

_____

✏️ When do you plan to work on this study? What time of day will work best for you?

_____

_____

✏️ What is today's date? _____ Take a few moments to journey to your Prayeramid (Appendix C).

Quotable

"Our wisdom, in so far as it ought to be deemed true and solid wisdom, consists almost entirely of two parts: the knowledge of God and of ourselves." John Calvin

Tuesday

Unit One • The Beginning of Wisdom

Beginning Your Relationships: Choosing Friends

Dig Site

Read Proverbs 1:8-19

Artifacts In Situ

- gun
- backseat
- bar stool

Today's Treasure

My son, if sinners entice you, do not give in to them.
Proverbs 1:7

"Drive! Drive! We shot a man!" shouted my friends as they scrambled down the street toward my car.

I gunned the engine and, without waiting for an explanation, spun the car around and headed in the very direction from which Jack and Danny had come.

"You fool! You're going to get us caught!" Danny yelled. The two men slumped in the backseat as several police cars and an ambulance sped into the supermarket parking lot, their lights flashing and their sirens blaring.

I made a right turn on Ponce de Leon Avenue — the only route I knew out of Atlanta — and took the Interstate north. For some time all I could hear was the rapid breathing of my friends in the backseat, and my head pounded with questions. 7

So begins the first chapter of *Twice Pardoned*, a book written by Harold Morris. Harold was an all-star athlete in high school, headed for a successful athletic career. Yet it was only a few years later when he found himself serving two life sentences in the Georgia State Penitentiary. What happened? If you ask Mr. Morris today, he will tell you that he was hanging out with the wrong friends.

It started by going to the wrong places, bars and clubs. He met the wrong kind of people there and started hanging around with them. As his story unfolds, we learn that Harold's "friends" implicated him with the crime they had committed. Falsely charged with armed robbery and murder, Harold was convicted and sent to prison.

Friends become especially important during your teen years. Your true friendships need to be built around like-minded people with similar values. Never underestimate the pull of your peers' approval. God can use your friends to call you to a closer walk with Him. The enemy can use your friends to distract you and tear your focus away from Christ.

Ask yourself these three questions about your current friendships:

1. Does this person encourage me in my walk with Christ?
2. Can I trust this person to give me godly advice when I have a problem?
3. Will this person be loyal to me through hard times as well as good times?

Look over these questions again. This time, ask yourself if you are the kind of friend you are looking for. Do you encourage your friends with kind words and a positive attitude? Are you faithful to support them in their Christian walk? Are you loyal?

As you go through life, you will have some friends who aren't Christians. That's okay. What's important is that you draw a line between acquaintances and intimate friends. God's Word clearly instructs Christians not to be unequally yoked together with unbelievers (2 Corinthians 6:14). Your true friends — the ones who spend the night at your house, the ones with whom you share your deepest thoughts — should be Christians. They are going to influence your life and inspire your living.

What about your non-Christian friends? Pray for them. Be there when they need you. Treat them as you would like to be treated. The Lord may lead you to establish a ministering friendship with an unbelieving young person and his family. As long as you and your family are influencing that guy for good, maintain the relationship. Feel free to share Christ with your friend. Invite him to church. However, if this friend shows no interest in Christ and you begin to see that he is dragging you down or causing you to act outside your family's acceptable scheme of things, then it's time to put some space in place. Ask God for direction and discernment in choosing friends.

How important are your friends? According to Harold Morris, your friends will determine the outcome of your life. That is a pretty strong statement. I have a feeling, though, that Mr. Morris is right. *"Don't let anyone deceive you. Associating with bad people will ruin decent people."*[8]

Data Entry

🖉 Is it hard to say "no" to your friends?

_____

_____

_____

🖉 Proverbs 1:10 encourages us not to give in when we are enticed. To entice means to attract, persuade, or tempt. What are some things that you know tempt you? Can you come up with a plan for not giving in the next time those things attract you?

_____

_____

_____

_____

🖉 List six qualities that you look for in a friend.

_____

_____

_____

Unearthing the Treasures of Solomon's Proverbs

🖉 As you look over the six qualities you listed, ask yourself which of the things you listed are traits that belong to you. Are you the kind of friend you're looking for? Be honest. What do you need to work on?

_____

_____

_____

🖉 What is today's date? _____ Take a few moments to journey to your Prayeramid.

Quotable

"Choose your friends carefully. Do they fear God? Do they receive the Word of God in their hearts? Use your friends' attitudes toward the Bible as an important test of friendship. Relationships are investments of our time and other resources. Make them count for eternity." Warren Wiersbe

Wednesday
Unit One • The Beginning of Wisdom

Beginning Your Teen Years: Wisdom's Cry

Dig Site

Read Proverbs 1:20-27

Artifacts In Situ

- coins
- war medals

Today's Treasure

Wisdom calls aloud in the street, she raises her voice in the public squares...
Proverbs 1:20

My friend John is an amateur treasure hunter. He uses a high-tech metal detector to search for coins, tokens, medals, and bits of jewelry. Living close to the site of a historical Civil War battlefield, John often spends time there, searching among tall grasses and brush. When he gets close to a bit of metal, the detector will begin to emit a series of beeps. The built-in computer program flashes instructions on a screen that tells John how deep to dig in order to find the "treasure." With his metal detector, John lets technology dictate whether he moves to the right or left when he is hunting for hidden treasures. It tells him when he is getting close to what he is looking for, and it lets him know when he has taken a wrong turn. The beeping sounds get louder and faster when he is zeroing in on a target. They grow faint and farther apart when he has missed the mark.

When you follow God's commands, it is not difficult to determine the right way. He has spelled it all out for you in His Word. Plus, if you are a Christian, you have the benefit of the Holy Spirit living inside you. He acts as somewhat of holy metal detector to keep you honing in on the real treasures of life. When you are faced with choices, He will let you know which way to go.

Unearthing the Treasures of Solomon's Proverbs

The book of Proverbs is all about how to make wise choices. Why does that seem to be such a difficult thing for people to do? People all over the world make poor choices every day, and they must live with the consequences of those decisions.

Solomon wrote, "Wisdom calls aloud in the street, she raises her voice in the public squares." Solomon made the point that Wisdom longs to get our attention. God has not hidden the right way from us. On the contrary, He has underlined it, circled it in red, and drawn stars out beside it. *Here it is! This is the way to go!* Admittedly, even when we know the right thing to do, it may not be so easy to actually DO it. God presents us with choices every day of our lives. Our selections will determine the quality of our lives.

Data Entry

✎ Write down Proverbs 1:20 here. Use any translation you like.

_____

_____

_____

_____

✎ How does wisdom "cry out" the obvious answer when it comes to smoking? Drinking? Doing drugs?

_____

_____

_____

✏️ What are some ways that God has used to point you in the right direction?

_____

_____

_____

_____

✏️ Read Appendix B, "Why Memorize Scripture?" Choose a passage to memorize. Write the reference of your selection here._____

✏️ What is today's date? _____ Take a few moments to journey to your Prayeramid.

Quotable

"Life is a series of choices between the bad and the good and the best. Everything depends on which we choose." Vance Havner

Thursday

Unit One • The Beginning of Wisdom

Beginning Your Life's Legacy: What Goes Around

The words "sowing" and "reaping" are words many guys today don't use very often. However, these terms are quite familiar to farmers and others who work with agriculture. When a person sows a seed, he is *planting* it. When that seed has produced, he "reaps" or *harvests* the crop it provided. Let's say that you wanted a garden full of tomatoes. Would you plant carrot seeds? Of course not! Sowing carrot seeds would only reap a garden full of delicious orange carrots. If you want tomatoes, you must sow the right seeds.

Scripture tells us the principle of sowing and reaping applies to all of life, not just farming. The apostle Paul explained it this way. He said, "Don't be misled: No one makes a fool of God. What a person plants, he will harvest. The person who plants selfishness, ignoring the needs of others — ignoring God! — harvests a crop of weeds. All he'll have to show for his life is weeds! But the one who plants in response to God, letting God's Spirit do the growth work in him, harvests a crop of real life, eternal life."[9]

One Friday morning, Sister Helen Mrosla, a Franciscan nun, was teaching her junior high math class when she noticed something didn't feel right. "We had worked hard on a new concept all week, and I sensed that the students were

Dig Site

Read Proverbs 1:28-33

Artifacts In Situ

⚑ notebook paper

Today's Treasure

. . . they will eat the fruit of their ways and be filled with the fruit of their schemes.
Proverbs 1:31

Dig Deep

frowning, frustrated with themselves — and edgy with one another," Sister Helen later wrote in an article for *Proteus* magazine.[10] "I had to stop this crankiness before it got out of hand."

She allowed the students to put away their math and take out two blank sheets of paper. "Then I told them to think of the nicest thing they could say about each of their classmates and write it down," she remembered. "It took the remainder of the class period to finish their assignment, and as the students left the room, each one handed me the papers." That weekend, the Sister wrote down the name of each student on a separate sheet of paper and listed what his or her classmates had said about each individual.

When the class reconvened on Monday, Sister Helen gave the students their lists. Everyone was smiling and encouraged over the positive comments they had received from their classmates. Sister Helen's brainstorm had accomplished the result she was hoping for: better attitudes that would allow a better atmosphere in which to learn math! She never dreamed of the far-reaching effects the lists would have until many years later, when one of the students in that junior high math class, Mark Eklund, was killed in Vietnam.

The Sister attended Mark's funeral, along with his family and his many friends, several of whom had been his math classmates. The former students invited her to join them at a restaurant after the burial. Mark's parents were there, too, waiting to see the Sister. They had something amazing to show her.

Taking a wallet out of his pocket, Mark's dad said, "They found this on Mark when he was killed. We thought you might recognize it." Opening the billfold, Mr. Eklund carefully removed two worn pieces of notebook paper that had obviously been taped, folded, and refolded many times. Sister Helen knew without looking that the papers were the ones on which she had listed all the good things each of Mark's classmates had said about him.

"Thank you so much for doing that," Mark's mother said. "As you can see, Mark treasured it."

When Mark's classmates gathered around the Eklunds and Sister Helen, they all admitted to keeping their lists, even after all those years. One man kept his in the top drawer of his desk; another had asked his wife to store his in their wedding album. One of the girls treasured hers so much that she kept it in her purse, carrying it with her at all times.

Sister Helen had encouraged her students to sow seeds of kindness with their thoughtful words and compliments toward each other. It paid off in a harvest that was reaped year after year as those lists offered encouragement every time they were read.

Even the non-Christians in our world believe you reap what you sow. A popular expression in today's world is, "What goes around, comes around." Sooner or later, a bully will wind up getting bullied by someone bigger and meaner. One day, the snob will get snubbed. The person who makes jokes at the expense of others will find himself laughed at in the end. The person who sows love, however, will be loved in return. The one who seeks to encourage with a kind word will find himself encouraged when he needs it. And the man who gives freely with no regard for himself will find he is living the greatest life of all. In the thousands of years that the earth has existed, nothing has altered the principle of sowing and reaping. Nothing ever will.

Data Entry

How would Sister Helen's story be different if the students had written rude or sarcastic comments about their classmates?

_____
_____
_____
_____

What if your siblings had a list of every comment you have ever made with regard to them? Would they want to carry that list with them forever?

_____
_____

✏️ What are you sowing into the lives of your siblings? If you continue in this manner, what will you reap?

_____
_____
_____
_____
_____

Sow a thought, reap an act;
Sow an act, reap a habit;
Sow a habit, reap a character;
Sow a character, reap a destiny. ~Aristotle

✏️ Copy the above quote by Aristotle here.

_____
_____
_____
_____

✏️ Work on your passage for memorization.

✏️ What is today's date? _____ Take a few moments to journey to your Prayeramid.

Quotable

"Proverbs gives us a long list of sins that get us into trouble, such as impatience, dishonesty, selfishness, a hot temper, and even talking too much. It also tells us that wisdom will keep us out of trouble. Anytime we ignore God's principles, we eventually suffer the consequences. We always reap what we sow." Rick Warren

Unearthing the Treasures of Solomon's Proverbs

Friday

Unit One • The Beginning of Wisdom

Lab Work: Artifacts and Heartifacts

⇨ Read back through Proverbs 1 and your data entries for this week.

⇨ Complete any unanswered questions from this week's lessons.

⇨ What will last from your study of Proverbs 1? List this week's Artifacts and Heartifacts below.

Artifacts

_____

_____

_____

_____

Heartifacts

_____

_____

_____

_____

⇨ Do some soul-searching about what God is teaching you. Record your thoughts below.

_____

_____

_____

_____

⇨ Work on your Scripture memory passage. You can do it!

⇨ Take a few moments to journey to your Prayeramid.

⇨ Don't forget this week's EXTRA! Watch "Twice Pardoned: An Ex-Con Talks to Parents & Teens."

| **Preview** | Unit Two • Facets of Wisdom |

Monday

Parental Wisdom: Listening to Love and Experience

Tuesday

Protective Wisdom: His Presence in the Storm

Wednesday

Discerning Wisdom: When the Buzzer Goes Off

Thursday

Life Wisdom: The Walk of the Righteous

Friday

Lab Work: Artifacts and Heartifacts

This Week's EXTRA

Using a local or national newspaper, newsmagazine, or website, find a current article about a Christian (celebrity, athlete, or Everyday Joe) who is choosing to stand up for what he/she believes in, despite the culture and popular opinion. Make a copy and paper clip it to this week's Lab Work page.

Monday

Unit Two • Facets of Wisdom

Parental Wisdom: Listening to Love and Experience

Dig Site

Read Proverbs 2:1-8

Artifacts In Situ

- duffle bag
- beach towel

Today's Treasure

. . . for he guards the course of the just and protects the way of his faithful ones.
Proverbs 2:8

"Go get help! Hurry!" Mike screamed to the others. As he treaded water at the bottom of the falls, he held on to Tyra, trying to help her keep her head above the water. "My legs!" Tyra cried.

It was the annual youth trip to the falls, and before 14-year-old Mike had left, his father had warned him. "Don't you jump off the falls like those kids did last year! They could've gotten killed!" The year before, there were some kids who jumped off the 90-feet-high falls. It had seemed pretty cool when they returned talking about it. But their youth minister didn't think it was very cool. This year, he had issued stern warnings as the youth piled on the church van with their Bibles and duffle bags. There was to be no jumping off the falls.

Mike had little time to think as he and another boy got Tyra over to the shore and wrapped a towel around her shoulders. As they sat waiting for the paramedics to arrive, however, he had plenty of time to consider the consequences of his decision to disobey. If he hadn't jumped, Mike realized, Tyra wouldn't have jumped. She wouldn't be crying now, with blistered, bruised legs from where she had landed at the bottom of the falls. So why did he do it? Sheepishly, Mike had to

Dig Deep

admit to himself it was because two of his friends did. "C'mon," they had urged, as they sneaked away from the group. "We've already done it once and it was a blast!"

If only he had refused. He felt that check in his spirit; he remembered what his dad had said. But he went anyway, unaware that Tyra had been watching him and the other guys. He had no idea she was following him as he followed his buddies. And then she jumped over the falls right behind him! It had all happened so fast! Now she was hurt — badly hurt — crying and everything.

Mike had seen the falls and knew they were dangerous. He had heard the warnings of his father and his minister, yet it was important to him to keep up with his friends.

You can get in a lot of trouble trying to keep up with your friends. Guys are naturally competitive. As a matter of fact, you were wired by God for risk and adventure. But don't confuse that with thrill-seeking and circus stunts. God made you with a sense of boldness and adventure in order to further His kingdom!

Christian recording artist Randy Stonehill wrote about God's desire to channel the boldness of young men into a godly passion for Christ in the song, "Angry Young Men."

He wants some angry young men

Ones who can't be bought

Ones who will not run from a fight

Ones who speak the truth

Whether it's popular or not

Ones who'd give up anything to walk in His light

Rest assured, when Jesus comes again

He'll be looking for some angry young men[11]

It takes a lot of guts to go against the crowd. It takes courage to give up your life to a God you can't see. It takes a daring heart to live as the disciples did — at the feet of Jesus, ready to take off at a moment's notice. It takes a man who can put his faith and trust in the one and only Jesus Christ.

Sometimes it's difficult to understand why parents do the things they do or ask the things they ask of you. In today's Scripture reading, we find wise King Solomon pleading with his son to accept his commands. More often than not, parents' instructions come from their life experiences. Your parents have been around a lot longer than you have. They have made lots of mistakes and learned from them. They know your actions affect not only yourself, but others who are following in your steps.

Data Entry

✎ Do you ever try to "outdo" your friends? How do you feel when you win at something? How do you feel when you lose?

_____

_____

_____

_____

✎ What do you do when you disagree with your parents? Do you react in a godly manner? What should you do?

_____

_____

_____

_____

✎ Look at Proverbs 2:4. How can you compare your parents' instruction to a "hidden treasure"?

_____

_____

_____

✏ Spend some time digging around your dad's life. Ask him about a time he didn't obey his parents and what happened. Jot down your comments here.

_____
_____
_____
_____
_____
_____

✏ Work on your passage for memorization.

✏ What is today's date? _____ Take a few moments to journey to your Prayeramid.

Quotable

"Children, obey your parents in the Lord, for this is right. 'Honor your father and mother' — which is the first commandment with a promise — 'that it may go well with you and that you may enjoy long life on the earth.'" St. Paul

Tuesday

Unit Two • Facets of Wisdom

Protective Wisdom: His Presence in the Storm

Dig Site

Read Proverbs 2:9-15

Artifacts In Situ

- street sign
- mailbox

Today's Treasure

Discretion will protect you, and understanding will guard you.
Proverbs 2:11

One spring night when I was young, a terrible storm came whipping through Nashville. At that time of year, serious thunderstorms can hit middle Tennessee, often developing into tornadoes. In our neighborhood there was a power outage, and unfortunately, we didn't have a battery-powered radio that would have provided us with updates on storm conditions. During severe weather, people are advised to seek shelter in an underground basement or in the innermost part of a building, away from windows. Since we didn't have a basement, my parents, my sister, and I gathered in the hallway, the safest place in our house, to wait out the storm.

We crouched together there, listening to the howling wind outside. I couldn't see anything, and I hated that. I think I was more scared of the dark than of the storm! I started to wonder if Mom and Daddy were really there in the hallway with us. I got very still and quiet. I could hear the storm raging all around, but somehow, above the storm, I could hear my dad's steady breathing, calm and assured. I couldn't see him, but I knew that he was there. I could feel him. His presence was strong and comforting, and even though he didn't say anything, I knew that everything was going to be all right.

As rain continued to pelt the roof and lightning danced outside, Mom asked Daddy, "Well, what do you want to do? There's no telling when they will get the power back on."

Daddy replied, "Let's pray and then go to bed. It's late — already past the girls' bedtime." We bowed our heads together. Daddy prayed for protection from the storm. He asked God for a good night's rest. He just prayed a simple, trusting prayer. Then he and Mom helped my sister and me find the way to our beds. We went to sleep in the middle of the storm.

When we awoke the next morning, my family went through the usual morning routine of eating breakfast and getting dressed for school. It wasn't until we got in the car and began backing out of the driveway that we even realized the effect of my dad's faith-filled prayer.

As we looked through the car windows at our neighborhood, we saw that during the night trees — huge weeping willow trees — had been uprooted. Up and down the street, their huge trunks lay like flatlines in people's yards. The giant hand of the storm had ripped the trees from the ground. Some roads were impassable. From homes and vehicles to mailboxes and street signs, storm damage was everywhere. It was everywhere, that is, except at our house. Our home was fine; our lawn was neat. Our yard displayed, incredibly, a clearly marked boundary of prayer.

God's Wisdom offers you the benefit of knowing what to do in the middle of the storm. The passage you read for today explains that our God gives wisdom, knowledge, and understanding. He is our guard through the storms, and He is also our guide. We are protected by our Lord.

Does that mean that life will be easy? No.

Does that mean that nothing bad will happen? No, not necessarily. What it means is that we can trust the Lord to be there, beside us, no matter what.

You may not be able to see Him.

You may not hear Him saying anything. You may only be able to hear the storm raging all around you.

Unearthing the Treasures of Solomon's Proverbs

However, if you get very still and quiet, you will be able to feel His presence. You will hear the whisper of His breath above the howling winds, and you will *know* He is there.

Data Entry

✎ What are you afraid of?

_____

_____

✎ Can you remember a time when God protected you from danger?

_____

_____

_____

✎ Are there times when you don't *feel like* God is with you? What would you tell a friend who said, "I don't think God cares about me?"

_____

_____

_____

✎ Work on your passage for memorization.

✎ What is today's date? _____ Take a few moments to journey to your Prayeramid.

Quotable

"Peace I leave with you; my peace I give to you. I do not give to you as the world gives. Do not let your hearts be troubled and do not be afraid." Jesus Christ

Wednesday

Unit Two • Facets of Wisdom

Discerning Wisdom: When the Buzzer Goes Off

Dig Site

Read Proverbs 2:16-19

Artifacts In Situ

- steering wheel

Today's Treasure

None who go to her [the adulteress] return or attain the paths of life.
Proverbs 2:19

My friend Wendy was a cute, outgoing blond with a knack for making friends. Her bubbly personality captivated everyone she met. As a college student, Wendy enjoyed going to night clubs with her friends. Her enthusiasm for life showed in her lively moves on the dance floor. Wherever she went, Wendy always got the attention of the club's band members, and her circle of friends was forever growing.

When Wendy became a Christian, the Holy Spirit moved into her heart and began to show her that certain things were hindering her Christian life. Determined to pursue Christ, Wendy quit drinking. When she told her friends about her decision, she noticed that only a few of them supported the choice she had made. Rather than lose friends, she began to keep quiet about her relationship with Christ. She didn't think God would want her to quit having fun, so she continued going out with her friends on the weekends. She became the "designated driver" so she could have an excuse for not drinking and be sure her friends got home safely.

This arrangement seemed like it was going to work for Wendy. She was able to have fun and go dancing with her friends, and she didn't bother them with the details of her new life with Christ. One day, however, Wendy came to me with a serious question.

"Rebecca," she said, "I just don't feel right when I go out with my friends anymore. They talk about things that I'm not interested in, and they don't want me to talk about the Lord. I want to have fun, but it's not fun anymore. What's going on?" As I pressed Wendy for more details, she shared that she felt the most uncomfortable when her friends in the band played a song they had written. It was a crowd favorite, but the song was full of obscene language — a foul message repeated over and over.

I knew the Holy Spirit would bless Wendy with a spirit of **discernment** if she would only ask for it. What is discernment? Author Neil Anderson explains:

> Discernment...[is] that "buzzer" inside, warning you that something is wrong. For example, you visit someone's home and everything appears in order. But you can cut the air with a knife. Even though nothing visible confirms it, your spirit detects that something is wrong in that home. The first step to understanding discernment is to understand the motive which is essential for employing [using] it. In 1 Kings 3:9, Israel's king Solomon cried out to God for help. God answers: "Because you have asked this thing and have not asked for yourself long life, nor have asked riches for yourself, nor have you asked for the life of your enemies, but have asked for yourself discernment to understand justice, behold, I have done according to your words. Behold, I have given you a wise and discerning heart" (verses 11, 12). The motive for true discernment is never to promote self, to amass personal gain, or to secure an advantage over another person — even an enemy... **Discernment has one primary function: to distinguish right from wrong.**[12]

"Wendy," I said, "ask God to show you what is really going on in that club. He will."

The next time Wendy went to the night club, she quietly bowed her head and asked God to show her the truth about the club and whether or not it was okay for her to be there. When she lifted her head, she saw a murky black cloud filling up the room. No one else noticed its suffocating presence. Wendy watched as the entire room was covered by a blanket of blackness. After a few seconds, the inky darkness faded away. Wendy told me she recognized immediately that God was showing her the presence of evil in the room.

You may not have an experience as dramatic as Wendy's, but there are many times when you will hear that "buzzer" going off in your heart. Will you listen to God when He prompts you to make good choices? When the buzzer goes off, be obedient. God has big plans for your life.

Data Entry

Have you ever heard the "buzzer" go off? What happened?

_____

_____

_____

Are there any people or places that make you feel uncomfortable? Do you think that God is trying to tell you something?

_____

_____

_____

What would you tell Wendy to do about her friendships?

_____

_____

_____

🖉 Work on your passage for memorization.

🖉 What is today's date? _____ Take a few moments to journey to your Prayeramid.

Quotable

"Discernment is not a function of the mind; it's a function of the Holy Spirit which is in union with your soul/spirit. When the Spirit sounds a warning, your mind may not be able to perceive [or make out] what's wrong. Have the courage to acknowledge that something is wrong when your spirit is troubled." Neil Anderson

Thursday
Unit Two • Facets of Wisdom

Life Wisdom: The Walk of the Righteous

"Until There's a Cure" day is an annual event at Candlestick Park, home of the San Francisco Giants baseball team. Each year, during a pregame ceremony, the Giants demonstrate their support for finding and funding a cure for AIDS, a disease that has affected many lives. (For a definition of AIDS, see page 135.) The Giants players are supposed to pin AIDS awareness ribbons to their uniforms and join AIDS volunteers (many of whom are homosexual activists) on the field in a show of solidarity.

On July 28, 1996, relief pitcher Mark Dewey refused to participate. He had taken part the year before, but he now believed that was a mistake. There were things about the AIDS awareness programs (namely, the Safe Sex programs that encourage and even sanction homosexuality and promiscuity) which were troubling to him, a born-again Christian. He felt that showing his support for finding a cure would be or could be mistaken as a show of support for homosexuality and fornication.

Unfortunately, his authorities insisted that he run onto the field with the others. So he turned his AIDS ribbon sideways, making it resemble a Christian icthus, or fish symbol.

Dig Site

Read Proverbs 2:20-22

Artifacts In Situ

- ribbon
- baseball
- glove
- newspaper

Today's Treasure

For the upright will live in the land, and the blameless will remain in it; . . .
Proverbs 2:21

Unearthing the Treasures of Solomon's Proverbs

The media, along with the gay community, in San Francisco went ballistic. Some people called for the Giants to release Mark and no longer allow him to play for that ball club. In what could be the greatest irony of our culture, the very people who plead desperately for tolerance to be shown toward them are the same ones who refuse to tolerate beliefs that differ from their own. After being maligned by newspaper editorial columnists and insulted by caller after caller on radio talk shows for several days, Mark issued this written statement:

> I am writing in response to many articles, letters and calls concerning my actions on "Until There's a Cure" day. Much speculation has been made about my character, but very little is based on the intent of my heart. Everything I have done and said has been to express love and compassion for all people with AIDS, their friends and families, and those who have lost loved ones to the disease, without compromising the teaching of Scripture.
>
> I have no hatred or ill-will toward homosexuals; I have concern for all who have AIDS, and I am not opposed to the search for a cure or action taken by people for research. I do, however, hate sin, and the Bible clearly teaches that sexual immorality (fornication, adultery, homosexuality, etc.) is sin.
>
> I could not be involved with the ceremonies because sexual immorality was condoned and in some cases encouraged. I altered the ribbon for the same reason. I wore the ribbon like a fish to show my love and compassion for lives as well as for souls.
>
> All I did and said was out of love for God and for people. The bottom line is this. The deadly "disease" we are battling is sin (it kills body and spirit). ALL have sinned. There is a cure — the shed blood of Jesus Christ.

Mark closed his letter with the following verses:

> "And He said to them, 'But who do you say I am.'" Luke 9:20. "This is the question the Lord asks each one of us." Acts 20:24[13]

At some point or another, every Christian has to take a stand for what he believes in. It may not be in a large, public arena. It may be at a friend's house —

refusing to watch an inappropriate TV show or DVD. It may be as simple as turning down a cigarette, an alcoholic drink, or an illegal drug substance. It might mean turning a deaf ear to gossip.

When you look at Mark Dewey's story closely, you realize that it is in the everyday things when we are called to exercise our faith and stand on God's Word. After all, while Mark was a major league baseball pitcher at the time, which seems like a pretty cool job, it was just that: his job. He took a stand that, had he worked as a banker or a mechanic, would have gone unnoticed by the mainstream press. Yet hundreds of thousands of times every day, God calls His many children to step up to the plate and hit one out of the park — by simply making the right choice. It is the walk of the righteous, and it begins every morning, as soon as your feet hit the floor.

Data Entry

🖉 Why do you think people were so angry with Mark Dewey?

_____
_____
_____

🖉 Do you think Mark Dewey was prepared for how people would react to his decision?

_____
_____

🖉 Look up Matthew 5:10-12. Copy verse 11 here.

_____
_____
_____
_____
_____

✏ What are some ways that God has asked you to stand up for Him? What happened?

_____

_____

_____

✏ Work on your passage for memorization.

✏ What is today's date? _____ Take a few moments to journey to your Prayeramid.

Quotable

"The deadly disease we are battling is sin (it kills body and spirit). **All** *have sinned. There is a cure — the shed blood of Jesus Christ." Mark Dewey*

Friday

Unit Two • Facets of Wisdom

Lab Work: Artifacts and Heartifacts

➪ Read back through Proverbs 2 and your data entries for this week.

➪ Complete any unanswered questions from this week's lessons.

➪ What will last from your study of Proverbs 2? List this week's Artifacts and Heartifacts below.

Artifacts	**Heartifacts**
_____	_____
_____	_____
_____	_____
_____	_____

➪ Do some soul-searching about what God is teaching you. Record your thoughts below.

_____

_____

_____

➪ Work on your Scripture memory passage. You can do it!

➪ Take a few moments to journey to your Prayeramid.

➪ Don't forget this week's EXTRA! Using a local or national newspaper, newsmagazine, or website, find a current article about a Christian (celebrity, athlete, or Everyday Joe) who is choosing to stand up for what he/she believes in, despite the culture and popular opinion. Make a copy and paper clip it to this week's Lab Work page.

Preview

Unit Three • Wisdom along the Way

Monday
In All Your Ways: Acknowledging God

Tuesday
Give It Away: Tithes and Treasures

Wednesday
Out-of-the-Ways: Bypassing the Drive-Thru

Thursday
Neighboring Ways: Making a Difference

Friday
Lab Work: Artifacts and Heartifacts

This Week's EXTRA

Do something out of your way for a neighbor, family member, or friend. It doesn't have to be anything fancy. Wash a car, write a note, or sweep a front porch.

Monday

Unit Three • Wisdom along the Way

In All Your Ways: Acknowledging God

What does it mean to *acknowledge* God? The online Merriam-Webster dictionary defines *acknowledge* with several meanings:

1: to recognize the rights, authority, or status of
2: to disclose knowledge of or agreement with
3a: to express gratitude or obligation for b: to take notice of c: to make known the receipt of
4: to recognize as genuine or valid

This dictionary further explains the word in this way, "*Acknowledge* implies the disclosing of something that has been or might be concealed."

Our relationship with God and our faith in Him are things that we might be able to conceal. Think about it. We don't have to let on that we are Christians. If you get too much money back from a cashier, you can cleverly conceal Christ's effect on your life by simply keeping the change. When your friends are making fun of someone you don't like anyway, you can hide God's love by going along with it. Those times when your siblings are really getting on your nerves, you can completely bury your Christian witness by blowing your top. But be warned: If we don't acknowledge God, we aren't admitting His presence in our lives. If we don't admit His presence, we limit His power.

Dig Site

Read Proverbs 3:1-8

Artifacts In Situ

- small change
- wooden plaque
- granite monument

Today's Treasure

Trust in the Lord with all your heart and lean not on your own understanding; in all your ways acknowledge him, and he will make your paths straight.
Proverbs 3:5-6

Unearthing the Treasures of Solomon's Proverbs

Now, I'm not talking about verbally confessing to every person you pass by, *Hey! I'm a Christian! God is at work in my life!* St. Francis of Assisi said, "Preach always; when necessary, use words." We can acknowledge the presence of God by our attitude, our actions, and our admission — in the everyday details of our lives — that we belong to Christ. Sometimes we will use words. Sometimes we won't.

For years, Judge Roy Moore of Alabama kept a hand-carved wooden plaque of the Ten Commandments hanging outside his office door. He believed that the Lord had put him in the office of judge, and he chose to honor God and acknowledge Him in this way. Some time later, Judge Moore chose to once again publicly acknowledge his faith and his allegiance to Almighty God by erecting a 5,200 pound granite monument of the Ten Commandments in the rotunda of the Alabama state Supreme Court building.

Judge Moore was asked to remove the monument. Initially, he refused because his interpretation of the Constitution provided him the freedom to display the Ten Commandments. However, after many court battles and appeals, along with a national controversy, the monument was indeed removed. But Judge Moore acknowledged God. I believe the Lord God acknowledges Roy Moore, too. He is blessed among men for what he did in taking a stand for the Lord.

It's not going to be easy to *acknowledge* God in all of your ways. The world and culture you live in want to deny the presence of God. God is a bother and an inconvenience to a selfish society that lives to cry out, "Me first!" However, you can change your corner of the world. Begin by practicing today. In every situation, offer words of praise to the Lord who loves you and wants you to know He is there. When you acknowledge Him, He promises to make your paths straight. He will keep you on track!

Data Entry

🖉 Copy these sentences below: "If we don't acknowledge God, we aren't admitting His presence in our lives. If we don't admit His presence, we limit His power."

_____

_____

_____

_____

🖉 When is it easy to acknowledge God's presence?

_____

_____

_____

🖉 Whether you acknowledge God or not, He is always present. Have there been times in your life when you tried to ignore God, but deep in your heart, you knew He was still there? How did you feel?

_____

_____

_____

_____

_____

🖉 Work on your passage for memorization.

🖉 What is today's date? _____ Take a few moments to journey to your Prayeramid.

Quotable

"I ran across the Ten Commandments that I had carved by hand some ten years earlier. I would have been quite hypocritical not to acknowledge the One who had placed me in office, so I hung them on the wall. I knew they would be controversial, but I did not suspect this would become a national controversy." Alabama Chief Justice Roy Moore

Tuesday
Unit Three • Wisdom along the Way

Give It Away:
Tithes and Treasures

What is the difference between an archaeologist and a treasure hunter?

Both research the sites they excavate.

Both seek items from the past.

Both remove objects from the ground and water.

A treasure hunter, however, searches only for objects that are valuable, while an archaeologist is interested in everything he finds. A tiny fragment of pottery is fascinating to an archaeologist because of what it tells him about the culture he is investigating. The same fragment would be discarded by a treasure hunter who is looking for gold, jewels, or collectible pieces like arrowheads or old coins. A treasure hunter is looking for monetary treasure, something that will give him personal riches. An archaeologist is looking for the treasure of wisdom — clues to a past culture that can teach him truths about today.

A treasure hunter seems to have a "finders keepers" mentality. He is on the hunt for wealth and riches, and if he finds it, that means it is his. An archaeologist, on the other hand, must adhere to a strict code of ethics that ensures he

Dig Site

Read Proverbs 3:9-18

Artifacts In Situ

- coins
- paycheck
- mailbox

Today's Treasure

Honor the Lord with your wealth, with the first fruits of all your crops; . . .
Proverbs 3:9

understands that his findings do not belong to him. They are for the greater good of all people.

Today's Scripture reading begins with instructions to tithe and ends with the assurance of peace. Our money — our treasure — is an area that can be a source of chaos or a place of peace in life. The key to the direction it will take lies in understanding your money does not belong to you. Ultimately, all income and gifts come from God. We are called to be managers, or stewards, of the money that is entrusted to us, using it for the greater good.

In the early years of our marriage, my husband Rich and I gave a yearly gift of $25 to a missionary couple, Marc and Carol. It wasn't a lot of money, but after giving our regular tithe, we didn't have a lot to spare. I wanted to give more, but how? I was pregnant and working a temporary job. My husband and I planned for me to stay home once the baby was born. Our tight budget was about to get even tighter. Yet somehow, God led me to pray a crazy prayer. "Lord," I prayed, "if You'll give me $300, I will give it to Marc and Carol."

A few days later, my boss came to me with some unexpected news. For the past couple of months, my paychecks had been miscalculated. The company, she explained, owed me some money. How much? Guess. You're right. I received a check for approximately $300.

Now, here's what I hate admitting. I sent that money straight to Marc and Carol, but as I was putting it in the mailbox and raising the flag for it to be picked up, I began to struggle. I thought of all the things we needed for our new baby. I thought of the upcoming hospital bill that $300 would certainly help pay. And I hesitated. Then, fortunately, I remembered the truth: I asked God for $300 to give to our missionary friends. He provided it. This money was never mine.

God calls His children to show faith in Him by giving back to His work as our first priority. Do we do this because God needs our money? No. We give back to God as a way to honor Him, recognizing His provision. In truth, the other ninety percent of our money belongs to God just as much as the first ten percent. We are to manage it wisely.

Unearthing the Treasures of Solomon's Proverbs

When our baby was born, she came home to a nursery filled with every good thing. Rich and I were showered with gifts from friends and family. We didn't have to buy anything for her! Our needs were met in an incredible way by our Heavenly Father.

And what about the offering I sent? I received a letter from Marc several weeks after sending the check. He had been hoping to attend a conference for further mission training, but he was short $300. Rather then worrying about it, he had trusted God to provide the money if he was supposed to go to the training conference. The check God had me send came just in time.

Data Entry

✎ Why do you think it is difficult for people to maintain an attitude of peace when it comes to money?

_____
_____
_____

✎ Jesus taught about money in Matthew 6:19-24. Read through those verses and copy verse 21 here.

_____
_____

✎ Ask your parents or grandparents to tell you about a time in their lives when God miraculously provided for their needs. Record what they say here.

_____
_____
_____
_____
_____

_____

_____

_____

_____

_____

_____

_____

_____

_____

_____

_____

✎ Work on your passage for memorization.

✎ What is today's date? _____ Take a few moments to journey to your Prayeramid.

Quotable

"Our money and possessions don't belong to us; they belong to God. God has given us the authority to be stewards of our money and possessions, and the responsibility to faithfully manage them according to the principles in the Bible." Larry Burkett

Wednesday

Unit Three • Wisdom along the Way

Out-of-the-Ways: Bypassing the Drive-Thru

Remember the Bible story of the twin brothers, Jacob and Esau, found in Genesis 27? Esau was born first, if only by a few minutes. That guaranteed him the special privileges and advantages that belonged to a Jewish child who was the first-born son, among those, the birthright.

The birthright was a holy, sacred gift, determined by birth order, which was determined by God. It included receiving a double portion of the father's inheritance. The birthright could actually be withheld or transferred, usually at the father's discretion. No son in his right mind would ever do such a thing, until Esau. Esau transferred his birthright to his brother Jacob. He traded it, in fact, for a bowl of stew.

The Bible tells us that Esau had been hunting in the country all day. He was starving when he returned home. Jacob had been working around the tents all day and had a nice pot of soup simmering. Esau asked for a bowl of the stew. Jacob, well aware of the potential of his brother's ravenous appetite, answered, "First, give me your birthright." Esau was offered a choice. If he wanted a bowl of stew, he would have to pay for it with his birthright.

Dig Site

Read Proverbs 3:19-26

Artifacts In Situ

⚱ soup pot

Today's Treasure

My son, preserve sound judgment and discernment, do not let them out of your sight; they will be life for you, an ornament to grace your neck.
Proverbs 3:21

Just what went through Esau's mind when Jacob presented him with this "deal"? How did Esau make his choice? And why?

Most people make choices based on three factors:

▲ Convenience,
▲ Habit, and
▲ Appearance.

These factors can work independently, or they can combine to create a more powerful influence. For example, the success of the drive-thru window is due largely to convenience, habit, and appearance working together. It is extremely convenient to pick up a sandwich. Millions of people pick up a breakfast sandwich every day on the way to work; thus, it becomes a habit. The drive-thru has a beautiful, full-color sign, and the parking lot is clean. The window itself is sparkling. It has a pleasant appearance.

Most people don't stop to think about the consequences of their choices. In the case of the daily drive-thru customer, he isn't thinking about the fact that his tasty bacon, egg, and cheese biscuit has 31 total fat grams, 250 mg of cholesterol, and 1360 mg of sodium. This adds up to a poor health habit that will not be convenient when it manifests itself in physical problems later on.

Esau made a poor choice. He sabotaged his own future when he got swept up in the here and now of a whining, grumbling stomach. He reasoned angrily, "Look! I am about to die! What good is the birthright to me?" Was he really about to die? No. Was the birthright going to be a lot of good to him? Yes. But convenience, habit, and appearance got the best of Esau.

Jacob made Esau swear an oath to him, and the deal was made. The pact was permanent. A lasting trade of eternal significance changed Esau's life. What did he get in return? A bowl of lentil stew, or POTTAGE, a cheap, common food of no value. (The term pottage is used as slang in India to refer to anything that is worthless.) You could say that Esau traded his birthright for the convenience of ancient Middle Eastern junk food.

Unearthing the Treasures of Solomon's Proverbs

Our choices affect our lives on a daily basis. We choose what we are going to wear, what we are going to eat, and what we are going to watch on TV. We choose whom we are going to call, whom we are going to befriend, and whom we are going to avoid. We choose how we are going to act, how we are going to speak, and how we are going to treat our family members. In making our daily choices, let's be careful to take them step-by-step and bypass the drive-thru.

Data Entry

🖉 What are some important decisions you've made so far in your life?

_____

_____

_____

_____

_____

_____

🖉 It's easy to grab a quick, greasy meal at a fast food restaurant, but it's healthier to prepare a meal with fresh ingredients at home. Why isn't the right thing to do always the easy thing to do?

_____

_____

_____

🖉 Work on your passage for memorization.

🖉 What is today's date? _____ Take a few moments to journey to your Prayeramid.

Quotable

"As we trust God to give us wisdom for today's decisions, He will lead us a step at a time into what He wants us to be doing in the future." Theodore Epp

Thursday

Unit Three • Wisdom along the Way

Neighboring Ways: Making a Difference

By Mike Griffin[14]

Dig Site

Read Proverbs 3:27-35

Artifacts In Situ

- sewing needles
- soup cans
- doll

Today's Treasure

Do not withhold good from those who deserve it, when it is in your power to act.
Proverbs 3:27

I remember that hot August Day in 1961. My cousins, my sister, and I spent most of the summer at our grandparents' house. There were six of us in all, ranging in age from about three to ten. Our parents would leave us with Grandma while they went to their jobs during the day. My grandparents didn't have much, but we never really knew the difference. To us, our grandparents' house was a wonderful place where we were loved and accepted and cared for, albeit quite simply.

And we thought that old house on 22nd Street was a magical place. It had an old basement where we could play Hide-and-Go-Seek, an enormous tree that was perfect for climbing, and a large grassy field where we played baseball. What more could a kid want?

Air conditioning was experienced only in the large department stores or during the occasional adventure to the movie theater. It was hot, and the heat was something that on those summer days could drain even six energetic kids.

As we lolled about the house, a tapping at the screen door rattled the stillness. It might be a door-to-door salesman! In those days salesmen carried large suitcases filled with brushes or pots and pans or some other new gadget. We all knew our grandma had no money to buy the stuff they were selling, but it was fun to watch the man pull out all those neat brushes and brooms and show how they could "clean up the house in half the time." On very rare occasions, that tap at the door might be an uncle or an aunt who had a car and was offering to take us to get ice cream.

We all raced to the door. None of us was prepared for what we saw. A little woman was standing there. We were just kids, but we could tell by looking at her that she had seen hard times, very hard times. Her face was wrinkled, and her shoulders were hunched over. I remember most of all the expression on her face and in her eyes. It was as if she didn't want to see anymore. Even at the age of nine, I knew that to be the look of hopelessness. Her simple dress was patched and frayed. Her shoes had holes.

Behind her stood a little girl, maybe six or seven years old. She was dirty from following her mother about those hot streets. She had no shoes. She had no smile. I remember her hair being matted to her forehead by the sweat, which made little brown lines as it dripped through the dust on her face.

"Is your mother home?" the little lady asked in a weary voice.

"No, but my grandma is," replied my cousin, and off she ran to find Grandma.

The rest of us stood there at the door staring. We said nothing. We all wanted to do something, but we didn't know what to do.

Grandma soon hurried to the door, drying her wet hands in her apron as she walked. She pushed open the screen door and peered through her bifocal glasses at our visitors. Before Grandma could speak, the little lady reached into a brown paper bag and pulled out a red foil package. She opened the foil pouch revealing sewing pins and needles.

"Would you like to buy some pins?" she asked.

Grandma, somewhat surprised, her eyesight not the best, squinted to get a better look at the little girl and finally replied, "How much are they?"

The lady replied, "Oh, anything you can give me."

Now, we knew Grandma had no money. It took all of Grandpa's hard-earned paycheck just to cover the bills and buy the groceries. She went to the closet, and we all followed, wondering what she would do.

We watched her pull out her big, black, Sunday pocketbook. She dug in every little pouch and pocket and turned it upside down and shook it. She found one dime and two pennies in a crease in the bottom. Going back to the kitchen, she pulled out a large brown paper grocery bag. She filled it up with cans of tomato soup, potatoes, tomatoes, and beans from her garden, and biscuits she had made for supper.

She tucked a doll into the bag, carefully hiding the toy beneath the food. She had kept the doll, which had belonged to one of her children, on the mantle above the fireplace. And she had made a beautiful dress for it with leftover pieces of material from her sewing projects. We knew this doll was special to her; none of the girls ever played with "Grandma's doll."

Grandma went back to the front door and gave the lady the bag of groceries and the twelve cents. She said, "This is all I have. Please take it, but please don't make me take your pins."

"Thank you, ma'am," said the lady, barely able to speak. She turned and walked down the blistering street with the little girl silently following, but we barely saw them. We kids were watching our grandmother. We knew when she had her eyes closed and her mouth was moving quietly that she was praying. She acted as if she were watching the little family walk down the hill, but we knew she was praying for them.

We were in awe of our grandmother. Even at our young age, we knew we had witnessed what Jesus had said, "She has given more than all the others. She has given all she had."

Data Entry

✎ What touches you most about this story?

_____
_____
_____
_____
_____

✎ The narrator of this story, Mike Griffin, seems most affected by the fact that his grandma gave away her special doll. Why do you think Grandma wanted to give her doll to that little girl?

_____
_____
_____

✎ What is your most special possession? Would you be willing to give it away if God asked you to?

_____
_____
_____

✎ Work on your passage for memorization.

✎ What is today's date? _____ Take a few moments to journey to your Prayeramid.

Quotable

"You can give something. Somehow, giving reminds us that the world does not revolve around us and that no matter what our financial status is, someone always is in a much worse situation." Dave Ramsey

Friday

Unit Three • Wisdom along the Way

Lab Work: Artifacts and Heartifacts

⇨ Read back through Proverbs 3 and your data entries for this week.

⇨ Complete any unanswered questions from this week's lessons.

⇨ What will last from your study of Proverbs 3? List this week's Artifacts and Heartifacts below.

Artifacts	**Heartifacts**
_____	_____
_____	_____
_____	_____
_____	_____

⇨ Do some soul-searching about what God is teaching you. Record your thoughts below.

_____

_____

_____

_____

⇨ Work on your Scripture memory passage. You can do it!

⇨ Take a few moments to journey to your Prayeramid.

⇨ Don't forget this week's EXTRA! Do something out of your way for a neighbor, family member, or friend. It doesn't have to be anything fancy. Wash a car, write a note, or sweep a front porch.

Unearthing the Treasures of Solomon's Proverbs

Preview

Unit Four • Wisdom Takes the Gold

Monday
No Deposit, No Return: The Cost of the Crown

Tuesday
Practice Makes Perfect: An Unlikely Olympian

Wednesday
Cheaters Never Prosper: Wisdom Wins First Place

Thursday
It's How You Play the Game: A Gracious Victor

Friday
Lab Work: Artifacts and Heartifacts

This Week's EXTRA
Read a biography of Olympian and Christian missionary Eric Liddell, and/or watch the movie "Chariots of Fire" with your family.

Monday

Unit Four • Wisdom Takes the Gold

No Deposit, No Return: The Cost of the Crown

Dig Site

Read Proverbs 4:1-9

Artifacts In Situ

- glass bottle

Today's Treasure

Wisdom is supreme; therefore get wisdom. Though it cost all you have, get understanding.
Proverbs 4:7

Every four years, a special event takes place involving countries all over the world: the Olympics. The international games are a tribute to the ancient Greek philosophy that intelligence and athleticism should co-exist; in other words, the Greeks believed a strong body was just as important as a strong mind. The first games are believed to have taken place in 776 B.C. The original site of the games, Olympia, was discovered by a French monk in 1723. Over one hundred years later, teams of German archaeologists began intense work on the site. The Archaeological Museum at Olympia opened in 1982, showcasing fabulous collections of artifacts related to the games and ancient Greece.

If you have ever watched the Olympic games on television, you may have seen the thrilling moment when the winner is presented with a gold medal for first place. Second and third place winners also receive medals (silver and bronze). All three athletes then stand before the crowd while the winner's national anthem is played. I am deeply moved as I imagine what the winner must be feeling. All those years of sacrifice and dedication have paid off.

Unearthing the Treasures of Solomon's Proverbs

When the gold medallist is interviewed by the television commentators, you quickly learn that winning was not left up to chance. You will never hear a champion casually saying that his sport is a hobby or something he does in his spare time. Whether on an ice rink, on a race track, or in a swimming pool, every winner has one thing in common: he has given his life in pursuit of the gold. What could possibly motivate a person to make that kind of trade?

John Naber captured five medals (four gold and one silver) at the 1976 Olympics. A competitive swimmer, Naber broke four world records that year. Here is his story.

> I was enjoying a bottle of root beer from an ice-filled Styrofoam chest. When I pulled out the glass bottle, the label came off but four words remained visible which taught me a life-changing lesson.
>
> The words said simply, "No Deposit, No Return."
>
> To enjoy the flavor inside, I had to pay the price. I had to invest in my dreams, if I wanted to see those dreams come true. I'm certain the maker of that bottle was thinking something else, but to this impressionable eleven year old, the words carried a lot of weight. I thought to myself, what am I depositing, in order to see my dreams come true? What price am I willing to pay?
>
> Every Olympian feels the same way. It is the act of paying the price "up-front," the willingness to invest in ourselves, the understanding that we have to feel tired in order to get stronger, which has allowed us to reach the medal platform. Some call it delayed gratification. I call it common sense.
>
> In the course of my career, (swimming ten miles per day, six days per week, eleven months a year) I traveled the equivalent of twice around the planet's equator. Each winter morning I walked across an ice-covered cement deck, steam rising from the pool's surface, bleeding the top three inches of water of their treasured temperature. The first swimmer in the pool (usually me) was the "ice-breaker" stirring up the water for the guys who followed. They often teased me about my eagerness because I sprinted the warm-up, crammed

the "free-swim" periods with thousands of yards and was often the last one out of the pool.

Viewed from the perspective of a deposit or an investment, the long hours in a pool or weight room were no longer a punishment, sacrifice, penalty or even an inconvenience. The hours spent now seemed like an investment in my future.[15]

In your Scripture reading today, King Solomon admonishes his sons to get wisdom and pursue understanding, "though it cost all you have." Have you ever considered that godliness comes with a price? Of course, salvation is God's free gift to us. Jesus Christ paid the price for our sins so that we wouldn't have to. But godliness — becoming a truly godly young man — that is costly.

Jesus said, "Don't look for shortcuts to God. The market is flooded with sure-fire, easygoing formulas for a successful life that can be practiced in your spare time. Don't fall for that stuff, even though crowds of people do. The way to life — to God! — is vigorous and requires total attention."[16]

Data Entry

🖉 Look up Jeremiah 29:13 and copy it here.

_____

_____

_____

🖉 An Olympic champion has sought the gold medal with his whole heart. How can you give your whole heart to pursuing God?

_____

_____

_____

🖉 What could your church family do and be if *everyone* made an Olympian commitment to pursue Wisdom, investing their lives in their church, community, and world? Think about this and write a 5-7 sentence answer.

_____

_____

_____

_____

_____

_____

_____

_____

_____

_____

_____

_____

_____

_____

_____

_____

✎ Work on your passage for memorization.

✎ What is today's date? _____ Take a few moments to journey to your Prayeramid.

Quotable

"I will not sacrifice to the Lord my God burnt offerings that cost me nothing."
King David[17]

Tuesday
Unit Four • Wisdom Takes the Gold

Practice Makes Perfect: An Unlikely Olympian

Wilma Rudolph was born in a tiny Tennessee town in 1940. She was the seventeenth of nineteen children. As a child, Wilma lived with poor health. She contracted double pneumonia and scarlet fever. Later, Wilma's body was diagnosed with polio. Her left leg began to atrophy, or weaken and deteriorate. Doctors told her family that Wilma would never walk again.

Dig Site

Read Proverbs 4:10-17

Artifacts In Situ

⚲ iron leg brace

Today's Treasure

When you walk, your steps will not be hampered; when you run, you will not stumble.
Proverbs 4:12

Although the doctors sent Wilma home wearing an iron leg brace, they didn't realize they were sending her home to a mother who didn't believe in the word "can't." The Rudolphs refused to believe the doctors. They determined that Wilma would walk again.

Wilma and her mother took a 50-mile bus trip twice a week for her treatment. (In those days of segregation, it was the closest hospital that would treat African-Americans.) After receiving physical therapy, Wilma went home and practiced on her own. Everyone in the large family took turns each day massaging Wilma's leg and helping her with exercises. Wilma's mother told her that with faith in God, the leg brace would one day come off. Wilma believed in God, and she believed in herself.

After spending two years bedridden, Wilma took her first step on her own when she was nine years old. By the time she was eleven, the leg brace came off.

What did Wilma do when she was finally set free from her limitations? She began to run. It was slow at first, but with practice and persistence, she soon began to run with the passion that had lain dormant in her heart for so many years. She lost many races, coming in last place, before she finally began to come in second to last. It wasn't long before Wilma was winning every race she ran.

In his book, *Something to Smile About,* Zig Ziglar writes, "At age 15, just four years after she threw away the brace, [Wilma] was invited by Ed Temple to train with the Tigerbelles, the celebrated Tennessee State University women's track team. At age 16, she qualified for the 1956 Olympic team but won only a bronze medal. She then enrolled at Tennessee State on a track scholarship and trained under Ed Temple, who coached the 1960 Olympic team. On that team Wilma became a superstar. On the day before her first heat in the 100, she severely sprained her ankle but still won gold medals in the 100 meter and the 200 meter. She then anchored the 400 meter relay en route to her third gold medal."

Wilma was blessed to have a mother who knew the value of godly wisdom. She knew that with God, nothing is impossible. She knew that her daughter could walk again with the Lord's help. She committed herself to encourage and assist her daughter, daring her to believe in a God she could not see or hear or touch. The apostle Paul wrote in the book of Hebrews, "Now faith is being sure of what we hope for and certain of what we do not see."[18] What Wilma could see was a mangled, withered leg. She could have put her trust in the doctor's hopeless diagnosis of a life spent crippled, but Wilma chose to follow Wisdom. She put her faith in a God whose healing hand she could not see, and Wilma Rudolph became an unlikely Olympian — the first woman to win three gold medals.

Wilma's story inspires me to believe that with practice, persistence, and passion, my dreams can come true and my deepest hopes can become reality. What are you dreaming of?

Data Entry

🖉 What if Wilma's mother had not encouraged her to have faith in God?

_____
_____
_____
_____

🖉 "You've got to put feet to your faith." What do you think this old saying means? How did Wilma and her family put feet to their faith?

_____
_____
_____
_____
_____

🖉 You have dreams of your own. Write down one of your dreams here. Make a list of steps you need to take to reach your goal.

_____
_____
_____
_____
_____
_____
_____
_____

_____

_____

_____

_____

_____

_____

_____

_____

🖉 Work on your passage for memorization.

🖉 What is today's date? _____ Take a few moments to journey to your Prayeramid.

Quotable

"What Wilma Rudolph did was incredible! I believe her success was not in spite of her problems, but because of them. She treasured the good health that others took for granted. Her joy filled her with an exuberance that intensified her training and enabled her to outshine the athletes of her day. Think about it. Follow your star, and chances are good you will reach new heights." Zig Ziglar

Wednesday

Unit Four • Wisdom Takes the Gold

Cheaters Never Prosper: Wisdom Wins First Place

In 1988 there was quite a scandal at the Olympic games. Runners Carl Lewis (American) and Ben Johnson (Canadian), long time rivals, were pitted against each other in the 100 meter race. Canada said that Ben Johnson was the fastest man in the world. The United States made that claim about Carl Lewis. The two had raced each other a total of fifteen times before the '88 Olympics held in Seoul, Korea. Carl had won nine of those competitions, and Ben had won six. As the young men lined up at the starting blocks, Americans held their breath to see who would win.

The winner was Ben Johnson. That day, the Canadian ran faster than any man in history. He ran 100 meters in 9.79 seconds. He broke every record that had ever been set. He was the fastest man in the world.

Two days after his victory, Ben Johnson was asked by the Olympics committee to take a drug test. He tested positive for drugs being in his system. He had been using steroid injections, carefully monitored by his trainer and a personal physician, to improve his performance. Ben's trainer, a man whom he trusted, had talked with him about using drugs to enhance his speed. He encouraged Ben, who was tired of being beaten

Dig Site

Read Proverbs 4:18-19

Artifacts In Situ

⚲ gold medal

Today's Treasure

The path of the righteous is like the first gleam of dawn, shining ever brighter till the full light of day.
Proverbs 4:18

Unearthing the Treasures of Solomon's Proverbs

by Carl Lewis time after time, that taking the steroids would give him the edge he needed to win. Ben decided to do it. He knew that drug use was illegal and that if he was ever caught, he would face severe punishment by the International Olympic Committee. Yet, knowing the risk, he took a chance — all for the sake of winning the gold.

Ben's coveted gold medal along with his record-breaking victory was stripped from him and given to Carl Lewis, who had come in second. Ben Johnson lost upwards of thirty million dollars in commercial endorsements. He was accused of betraying his country and became the butt of jokes — his name forever associated with "cheater" rather than "champion."

What motivated Ben Johnson to risk everything? Was it the money? Was it the fame? Was it the glory of winning? He pursued winning with passion, but he was willing to win in name only, knowing that he himself didn't win but that a chemical substance had won the race for him. What kind of a champion is that?

Wisdom calls us to the life of an AUTHENTIC champion. After all, Jesus is the real thing, and He calls us to a life of authenticity as well. There are plenty of people out there who are willing to be known for something they are not. As Christians, however, we are called to a life of character, not simply reputation. Someone once said, "Reputation is what others think of you. Character is who God knows you really are."

A champion friend won't cheat by breaking promises.

A champion son won't cheat by disobeying his parents.

A champion brother won't cheat by embarrassing his siblings around others.

A champion husband won't cheat by flirting with other women or dreaming about long-lost girlfriends.

A champion student won't cheat by copying off someone else's paper.

Cheaters never prosper. Eventually, they are found out. Scandal follows, as does shame. Victory comes when the gold is rightfully handed to the authentic champion.

Data Entry

🖉 Whom do you think of as an authentic Christian? (This needs to be a person that you know personally.) List some of this person's character qualities. Which of these qualities do you need to work on in your life? Ask God to help you.

_____

_____

_____

_____

🖉 What might have been going through Ben Johnson's mind when they came to take the gold medal away from him?

_____

_____

_____

_____

🖉 How do you think that Carl Lewis felt when he was given the gold medal?

_____

_____

_____

_____

✏️ Work on your passage for memorization.

✏️ What is today's date? _____ Take a few moments to journey to your Prayeramid.

Quotable

"Circumstances may appear to wreck our lives and God's plans, but God is not helpless among the ruins. God's love is still working. He comes in and takes the calamity and uses it victoriously, working out His wonderful plan of love." Eric Liddell

Thursday

Unit Four • Wisdom Takes the Gold

It's How You Play the Game: A Gracious Victor

Dig Site

Read Proverbs 4:20-27

Artifacts In Situ

- baseball

Today's Treasure

Above all else, guard your heart, for it is the wellspring of life.
Proverbs 4:23

The World Series is like the Olympics of Major League Baseball. And for the boys who play Little League Baseball every summer, they have their own Olympian-type event: the Little League World Series. This baseball tournament is held every August in South Williamsport, Pennsylvania. When it was first held in 1947, and for many years after, the competition was only between teams from the United States. However, the Series now truly lives up to its name and has become a world-wide baseball tournament for players under 13. It's usually broadcast on ESPN.

The summer of 2002, my family eagerly watched the United States team from Kentucky win the Little League World Series. I cheered enthusiastically for the incredible kids who had played their hearts out. We Powells felt a real connection with the team from Louisville because of our own Kentucky ties (and American pride, of course!). Watching the Series night after night, we felt like we got to know those boys and their coaches. Their personalities were revealed in their determination at the plate, their cheers from the dugout, and their concentration on the field. After all, even a child is known by his doing.

When Kentucky's pitcher Aaron Alvey realized his team had just won the Little League World Series, it was the greatest moment of his life. In the final game he had homered for the game-winning run. In the series itself, he set two pitching records for strikeouts and scoreless innings and tied the mark for consecutive no-hit innings. He was the victor! At the age of 12, this guy was sitting on top of the world.

While I watched ecstatically from my living room, the camera panned across the dugout where the Japanese team was sobbing uncontrollably. My enthusiasm simmered down as I realized that on the same field where there were excited winners, there were also disappointed losers. What would happen when those players were lined up for the traditional goodwill team walk? After every Little League game, the players of each team line up to shake hands. It is a sportsmanlike gesture that provides closure to the game. Would the losing Japanese team be able to extend their congratulations to the American winners? What would the Americans do when they saw all those tears?

Aaron Alvey led the Kentucky team to the field. I noticed a flicker of concern cross his face when he saw the other team crying with bitter disappointment. In what I believe to be an even greater moment of victory for Aaron Alvey, I watched as he reacted by doing something genuinely sportsmanlike and compassionate. Rather than only extending his hand, Aaron Alvey opened his arms. He hugged the Japanese players and patted their backs with careful respect. However exuberant he and his teammates felt inside, they showed a gracious humility when they realized their victory came at a heartbreaking price for the team that lost.

Such is the type of modesty displayed by a compassionate victor. Most of the time, this kind of winner has seen plenty of losses in his own life, and he knows well how to be sensitive to others. I'm sure that's why God allows losses in our lives. That's why He allows defeat, embarrassment, pain, and loneliness. These trials prepare us to minister to others. When the victories come along, as they most certainly will, we must never forget there are those on the perimeter who are suffering from sorrow.

Data Entry

✏ "I knew we could go somewhere, but I didn't think we could go this far," said Aaron Alvey after winning the Little League World Series. We've been talking about your dreams this week. You know you can go somewhere. Commit to God your highest hopes and dreams. Spend some time writing about how you want to "play the game."

_____
_____
_____
_____
_____
_____
_____
_____
_____
_____
_____
_____
_____

✏ Look up 2 Corinthians 1:14 and copy it here.

_____
_____
_____

🖉 What are some losses or disappointments you've gone through? Do you see how God can use your pain to comfort and minister to others?

_____

_____

_____

_____

_____

_____

_____

🖉 Work on your passage for memorization.

🖉 What is today's date? _____ Take a few moments to journey to your Prayeramid.

Quotable

"I have goals, but God has a plan. Whatever plan he has, whether I finish first place, third or twelfth, I do everything I can to satisfy God. We're always a winner in His book — regardless of how we do." Meb Keflezighi

Friday Unit Four • Wisdom Takes the Gold

Lab Work: Artifacts and Heartifacts

⇨ Read back through Proverbs 4 and your data entries for this week.

⇨ Complete any unanswered questions from this week's lessons.

⇨ What will last from your study of Proverbs 4? List this week's Artifacts and Heartifacts below.

Artifacts	**Heartifacts**
_____	_____
_____	_____
_____	_____
_____	_____

⇨ Do some soul-searching about what God is teaching you. Record your thoughts below.

_____
_____
_____
_____

⇨ Work on your Scripture memory passage. You can do it!

⇨ Take a few moments to journey to your Prayeramid.

⇨ Don't forget this week's EXTRA! Read a biography of Olympian and Christian missionary Eric Liddell, and/or watch the movie "Chariots of Fire" with your family.

Unearthing the Treasures of Solomon's Proverbs

Preview — Unit Five • Wisdom Defends His Honor

Monday

Exposing the Enemy: Death Dressed Up

Tuesday

Preparing for Battle: Staying Inside the Lines

Wednesday

A Word of Warning: Sex Has a Price Tag

Thursday

Warning Bell: Sounding the Alarm

Friday

Lab Work: Artifacts and Heartifacts

This Week's EXTRA

Visit your local crisis pregnancy center. Call ahead to let them know you are coming. Take a gift of diapers, wipes, or baby formula with you.

Monday

Unit Five • Wisdom Defends His Honor

Exposing the Enemy: Death Dressed Up

The entire fifth chapter of Proverbs deals with adultery. The dictionary defines adultery as: *sexual intercourse between a married person and someone other than his/her spouse.* If this is the case, then why is King Solomon taking such great pains to warn his son against adultery? Is the prince married?

God's Word defines adultery somewhat differently from the dictionary. The Jewish Law of the Old Testament takes the definition another step and calls it: *any unlawful sexual intercourse.* This would include fornication (sex between unmarried people), as well. Jesus then, when He was teaching the disciples one day, took the definition yet a step further.

"You have heard that it was said, 'Do not commit adultery.' But I tell you that anyone who looks at a woman lustfully has already committed adultery with her in his heart."[19]

So that means viewing pornography belongs in the definition of adultery, too. All manner of infidelity (disloyalty, marital unfaithfulness) is the kind of life, warns King Solomon, that leads to death.

Death?

Dig Site

Read Proverbs 5:1-6

Artifacts In Situ

⚲ magazine

Today's Treasure

For the lips of an adulteress drip honey, and her speech is smoother than oil; but in the end she is bitter as gall, sharp as a double-edged sword.
Proverbs 5:3,4

Satan dresses up sin. He glamorizes it. He makes sin look attractive and enticing. The word sensual has to do with fleshly appetites, be they for hunger, pleasure, or physical satisfaction. The world has targeted your sensual appetites and made everything under the sun easily available in order to satisfy them. As you grow into a man, you have to learn how to access what is easily available to you as a child of God: self-control. It is when a man does not control himself that he succumbs to the sensual, and to death.

Death by disease.

Death by guilt.

Death by shame.

Death by regrets.

Death by "what could have been," "if only," and "I wish I hadn't."

Don't be fooled by death dressed up!

Studies have shown that Christian young people are just as likely to participate in sex before marriage as non-Christian young people. Why is that? My pastor says it's because today's Christians, from teens to adults, are not in the Word of God. We're not reading our Bibles, and in many cases, our church leaders aren't reading their Bibles.

If you don't want to be captured by the sensual, then you must have a battle plan, and you must be wise to the enemy's tactics. Decide now that you will study God's teachings, follow God's teachings, and steer clear of adultery. That means refusing to look at pornography on the Internet or in magazines, even if everyone else is doing it. Even if you're at a friend's house and you think no one will ever know. Even if a relative or a good friend that you trust is the one who shows it to you. Run! Flee! It's death dressed up.

It means turning your eyes from girls who are immodestly dressed — on television, in catalogs, at the beach or pool, in classes, and even at church. Even if she wants you to look at her! Especially if she wants you to look at her. Remind yourself that you are looking at death — death dressed up.

Your best strategy means committing your purity to God, and cooperating with Him to establish a firm resolve that sex is for marriage, and your life belongs to Jesus. Don't waste your youth — your best years — doing anything less than serving Christ. You must set boundaries and build hedges, which we'll talk about more tomorrow.

You're not alone in this war, but sometimes it will feel as though you are. Make sure you spend time with the Lord every day, reading His Word and praying. He will expose the schemes of the enemy and provide you with the weapons necessary for victory.

Data Entry

🖊 Write down a definition of adultery using what you've learned from this lesson.

_____

_____

_____

🖊 Look up Romans 3:23. Copy it here.

_____

_____

🖊 Read Job 31:1-8. Would you prayerfully consider making a covenant with your eyes? If so, copy Job 31:1 below, and sign your name.

_____

_____

_____

✏ Work on your passage for memorization.

✏ What is today's date? _____ Take a few moments to journey to your Prayeramid.

Quotable

"At first all this was just a game to me, just another way of entertaining myself. But finally I realized the cycle of porn, lust, and sexual fantasies had me in their grip. My personal life was spinning out of control, and I knew that given the opportunity, I would do something that would destroy my marriage." Clay Crosse

Tuesday

Unit Five • Wisdom Defends His Honor

Preparing for Battle: Staying Inside the Lines

Dig Site

Read Proverbs 5:7-14

Artifacts In Situ

- hedge clippers

Today's Treasure

Keep to a path far from her, do not go near the door of her house, lest you give your best strength to others and your years to one who is cruel. . .
Proverbs 5:8,9

When I was a child growing up in Nashville, Tennessee, I remember watching my dad as he took care of our landscaping. We had a roomy corner lot, and Daddy took an artistic pride in the many shrubs and bushes that were on our property. A beautiful, lush, green hedge separated our yard from our next door neighbor's, and I remember the many times I watched my dad work on it. This was long before electric gardening tools became available. My dad used a large pair of manual hedge clippers, and he barbered those bushes with skilled expertise! They were impeccably crafted by the time he was finished, cut in perfect boxes with magnificent ninety-degree angles on every side. Daddy's hedges hemmed in the boundaries of our yard. But the pride he took in them caused them to be more than mere margins — they were masterpieces!

Jerry Jenkins (you may know him as the author of the *Left Behind* book series) believes that hedges need to be erected in our lives in order to create boundaries around our sexual purity. This goes for teens as well as adults, single people as well as married couples. We set up our boundaries, or limitations, and then we tend to them. We take pride in them. Now is the time to decide where to plant your hedges.

God's Word is a great place to start. The Bible makes it clear that sexual sin, whether it's before marriage or after marriage is wrong. Your first hedge should be saving sex for marriage.

Unfortunately, you are living in a sex-crazy world. Fornication, or sex before marriage, is totally accepted by our sinful society. In fact, as you get older, you will find that the approval of fornication is one of Satan's most widely accepted false teachings. *Sex before marriage is okay,* he says. *Everyone does it.* And indeed, it does seem like everyone does, but that's not true.

If you listen to secular radio stations and music by groups that aren't Christian, then you will probably hear a lot about sex. Watching television shows and even the commercials could also lead you to believe that everyone is having sex without the benefit or commitment of marriage. But keep in mind, those songs and TV shows are godless. There is no mention of God, so why should there be any adherence to His laws? Maybe you need to plant a hedge around your entertainment choices.

Sexual sin is in many ways different from other sins. Sex involves your body, your mind, and your emotions. Sexual sins linger; you carry them with you into adulthood. The least of these consequences would be unpleasant memories and bitter regrets. The worst would be contracting sexually transmitted diseases that can lead to infertility (being unable to biologically father a child) or even death.

Plant your hedges. It's never too early. As you plant them, keep in mind that they must be carefully tended. You have an enemy that will test your hedges. The devil wants to see just how serious you are. Will you be diligent to guard for weeds that might want to creep in and overtake your hedges? Cut things and people out of your life that cause your boundary lines to become blurry. Your life is wonderful! The hedges you plant out of obedience to God are beautiful. God will bless you through your hedges. I promise!

Data Entry

✏ Write down a few hedges you want to plant around your sexual purity. Ask God to bless your hedges and make them a beautiful witness of His love.

_____
_____
_____
_____

✏ Find Psalm 119:9. Copy it here.

_____
_____
_____

✏ How will you respond to friends who don't understand the hedges you have planted? How will explain your choices?

_____
_____
_____

✏ Work on your passage for memorization.

✏ What is today's date? _____ Take a few moments to journey to your Prayeramid.

Quotable

"Why [is] it so important that people not commit adultery? I submit that the reasons, whatever they are, are the same reasons we need to build hedges around our hearts, eyes, hands, spouses, and marriages. If adultery is in the same class as murder, it is a threat not only to our marriages but to our very lives." Jerry Jenkins

Wednesday
Unit Five • Wisdom Defends His Honor

A Word of Warning: Sex has a Price Tag

By Pam Stenzel[20]

You won't believe what I discovered during the nine years that I counseled girls who came into my pregnancy counseling offices in Chicago and Minneapolis. Most were worried sick about being pregnant. Very few were concerned about the venereal disease epidemic that is sweeping America.

Girls would come to my office and say: "Pam, if I had known this was going to happen to me, I would have made a different choice. But no one told me." I began to ask these girls: "What could we have told you? What could someone have shared with you, before you made your choice?" After all those years I realized there are a lot of students making decisions about sex who have no idea what the consequences of their decisions will be. I am writing this so that none of you will ever again be able to say to a physician, a counselor, or to your future husband or wife: "Nobody told me. I didn't know."

Girls Hope They're Off The Hook

Most teens who are having sex are afraid of getting pregnant. Girls come into my office for pregnancy testing, and when I tell a girl her test is negative, she gets a look of relief over her face,

Dig Site

Read Proverbs 5:15-20

Artifacts In Situ

⚲ pregnancy test

Today's Treasure

May your fountain be blessed, and may you rejoice in the wife of your youth.
Proverbs 5:18

as though to say: "I'm off the hook. I'm not pregnant. Let me out of your office." Wait a minute! Have you been tested for syphilis, gonorrhea, herpes, Chlamydia, trichinoma, vulvadema, urethritis, hepatitis B, HPV, or HIV? You have a four times greater chance of contracting a sexually-transmitted disease (STD) than you do of becoming pregnant.

For nine years I've also had to tell hundreds of girls their tests were positive — "You're pregnant." Immediately they want an easy, painless way out. I have to look at them and say: "Sorry. Your choices at this point are bad, terrible, and worse. You had a good choice before you chose to have sex. Now all of your choices are going to carry painful lifelong consequences."

Guys Pay Dearly Too

Guys are also facing very serious consequences for having sex outside of marriage. Lawmakers are now holding young men in this country responsible for having sex and getting a girl pregnant. The fact is, guys, it can cost you tens of thousands of dollars over the next eighteen years. The state you live in has the legal right to take away a sizeable portion of your pay from your job to support the child you fathered. If you're not yet working, you'll go into debt.

A young man I know who got a girl pregnant in Minnesota is being required by the State to pay $350 a month to support his little girl. That's based on his current income working at Burger King. "I made a decision one night after drinking," he said, "that I never would have made if I had been sober. And I will pay for that decision for the rest of my life." This is a very serious responsibility, young men. You need to think about that before you have sex, because after having sex, it's too late.

Venereal Disease Epidemic

Today, in the next 24 hours, 12,000 teenagers will contract an STD. And that's just teenagers. Looking at the entire population, there are about 50,000 people each day in our country who contract a sexually-transmitted disease. Yesterday, 12,000 of them were teenagers who got up in the morning like some of you reading this, and said: "It's not going to happen to me. That happens in big cities, but not where I live." Wrong!

Chlamydia Sterilizes

In the 1950's there were only five STDs that were known and treated. Today there are more than *fifty*. Chlamydia is the number one STD among teens today. There are about 4,000 teenagers every day who contract Chlamydia. This is a bacteria, not a virus.

Unlike some venereal diseases, it can be cured. But more than 80 percent of the students who contract this disease do not realize they have it. If you contract Chlamydia once in your life, you have a 25 percent chance of being sterile the rest of you life. If you get this disease more than once, the chances are much greater that you will never be able to have children.

At first, abstinence may sound negative, but it's a very positive choice that brings you freedom and peace of mind. Here's a good example . . . Five senior guys at a high school in Orlando, Florida, bought a full-page ad in their yearbook. They put pictures of themselves with their prom dates in the ad. The headline reads: "True Love Waits" and goes on to say, "We are making a statement to our fellow classmates that we will never abuse women, use them for sport and dump them. We are choosing to save sex for our wives."

Sex is not a game. But if you treat it like a game, it can have very harmful, long-term consequences. Sex was meant to be more than just a biological act. God meant sex to be a one-flesh experience — the bonding of two people physically, emotionally, and spiritually for life. When you abuse sex it doesn't just damage your body, it damages you, and it damages your partner.

Data Entry

✏ Pam Stenzel presents a lot of information in her article. Why is it important for a godly young man to be educated in regard to the worldly consequences of sin? Here are four reasons.

1. **To counsel others.** Read Psalm 127:3,4. Copy verse four here.

   _____

   _____

   _____

   A warrior doesn't store his arrows. He sharpens them, and then he sends them out into the world. As you become a wise man, you will find people seeking your advice. The world needs to know there are consequences to disobeying God's laws.

2. **To confirm the rightness of God's rules.** God's rules don't keep us from having fun. They are life-saving. Read 1 Corinthians 6:18-20. Copy verse 18 here.

   _____

   _____

   _____

   _____

3. **To expose Satan's lies.** Read John 8:44. Who does Jesus say the devil is?

   _____

   _____

   _____

Unearthing the Treasures of Solomon's Proverbs

4. **To be encouraged.** Knowing the truth about the consequences of an impure life will help you be steadfast in your decisions when you are tempted. Read Hebrews 10:23-24. Copy verse 23 below.

_____

_____

_____

_____

🖉 What is today's date? _____ Take a few moments to journey to your Prayeramid.

Quotable

"I made the decision as a teenager to be abstinent. I wanted to take control of my future. It wasn't a popular decision then, just like it can be an unpopular decision now. It doesn't always make me more friends. But the friends I have are true friends. True to themselves and true to me. We know each other's goals and dreams and we encourage each other to achieve them. It isn't easy. But every single day I say 'yes' to abstinence, it becomes that much easier. If you make a decision, and you practice it, that practice turns into a habit and the habit becomes a lifestyle." A. C. Green

Thursday
Unit Five • Wisdom Defends His Honor

The Warning Bell: Sounding the Alarm

Purity isn't just a state of body. It's truly a state of mind, as well. If we can somehow keep our minds pure, then it will be much easier to keep our bodies pure. Remember what you learned from Aristotle in Unit One, "Sow a thought, reap an act. Sow an act, reap a habit. Sow a habit, reap a character. Sow a character, reap a destiny."

God's Word tells us specifically how to think. In Philippians 4:8, Paul instructs the people. "Summing it all up, friends, I'd say you'll do best by filling your minds and meditating on things true, noble, reputable, authentic, compelling, gracious — the best, not the worst; the beautiful, not the ugly; things to praise, not things to curse."[21] These are also known as "things above."

When I was a young teen, I got my first baby-sitting job. The little boy was about six years old, and he was a lot of fun. He wanted to play hide and seek, so he ran to hide while I counted. His hiding place turned out to be the large, lighted closet of his mom and dad's bedroom. That's where I found him, crouching beside his dad's shoes, underneath a poster of a nude woman that was pinned to the wall.

Of course, I quickly got him out of the closet, gently asked him not to hide there again, and we resumed our game. But after I put him to bed for

Dig Site

Read Proverbs 5:21-23

Artifacts In Situ

- poster
- thumbtack

Today's Treasure

For a man's ways are in full view of the Lord, and he examines all his paths.
Proverbs 5:21

the night, I thought about that picture. And I wondered about a dad who would pin something like that on the wall.

Now, as an adult, when I think about that story, I wonder about some other things. I wonder what it was like for that little boy to grow up in a home thinking that pornography was normal. Since his daddy tacked pictures of naked women on the wall of his closet, he grew up thinking that all daddies — and therefore, all men — did. I wonder how the little boy's mom could walk by that picture day after day as she went to get her own clothes out of the closet. Why didn't she rip it down? Unless her dad did the same thing, and she thought that was what all daddies did.

The thing about having a picture like that in a closet is that God still sees it. The same is true with our minds. We can have thoughts and images taped up in the walls of our minds and think that they are there for our own viewing pleasure — that no one else can see them. But Someone can. He sees everything, and He charges us to keep our thoughts on things above.

How do you do that? First, you've got to avoid things that cause your mind to think on things below. That requires some self-study and self-examination. Ask God to show you where you're weak. He will. He wants you to get control of your thoughts and keep them pure. He's in this with you.

Second, have a plan of replacement thoughts. The Bible says to flee when we are tempted. If the temptation is in your mind, you need some thoughts you can flee to. In other words, when you find yourself thinking about things below, have something you can quickly substitute to get your mind distracted and occupied with something else.

▲ How about praying for other people? Keep a list of lost friends or family members in your mind and pray for them when you try to redirect your thoughts.

▲ How about praising God for His many holy characteristics? His faithfulness, goodness, mercy, and grace are worthy of our thoughts and our praise.

Dig Deep

▲ How about organizing a service project? Is there a ministry you could be involved in that would fill up your time and therefore your thoughts?

And really, the best thing to substitute is the Scripture verses you're trying to memorize. God's Word will take your mind and quickly set it back on things above.

Purity isn't a line you draw in the sand. It's a life you live between your ears! Guard your thoughts, and it will pay off in every other area of your life.

Data Entry

🖉 Many teens today get in trouble with their thought lives by the things they watch on TV and view on the Internet. How can you avoid these problems?

_____
_____
_____
_____

🖉 What are some things you can think about that would be honoring to God?

_____
_____
_____
_____

🖉 Copy Colossians 3:2 here.

_____
_____
_____
_____

🖉 Work on your passage for memorization.

🖉 What is today's date? _____ Take some time to journey to your Prayeramid.

Quotable

". . . the Bible teaches us in times of temptation . . . there is one command: Flee! Get away from it . . . for every struggle against lust in one's own strength is doomed to failure." Dietrich Bonhoeffer

Friday — Unit Five • Wisdom Defends His Honor

Lab Work: Artifacts and Heartifacts

⇨ Read back through Proverbs 5 and your data entries for this week.

⇨ Complete any unanswered questions from this week's lessons.

⇨ What will last from your study of Proverbs 5? List this week's Artifacts and Heartifacts below.

Artifacts	**Heartifacts**
_____	_____
_____	_____
_____	_____
_____	_____

⇨ Do some soul-searching about what God is teaching you. Record your thoughts below.

_____
_____
_____
_____

⇨ Work on your Scripture memory passage. You can do it!

⇨ Take a few moments to journey to your Prayeramid.

⇨ Don't forget this week's EXTRA! Visit your local crisis pregnancy center. Call ahead to let them know you are coming. Take a gift of diapers, wipes, or baby formula with you.

Unearthing the Treasures of Solomon's Proverbs

Preview — Unit Six • Wisdom Stays Out of Trouble

Monday

Mouthy Messes: Before It Gets Cold

Tuesday

Active Ants: High Hopes for the Greatest Generation

Wednesday

Terrible Troublemakers: 7 UPs God Hates

Thursday

A Real Relationship: Show and Tell

Friday

Lab Work: Artifacts and Heartifacts

This Week's EXTRA

Ask a grandparent or an older person you know what "work ethic" means. Ask him or her how the work ethic of our country has changed (or if it has). Record this person's thoughts on this week's Lab Work page.

Monday
Unit Six • Wisdom Stays Out of Trouble

Mouthy Messes: Before It Gets Cold

Your Scripture reading for today discusses the trouble that our tongues can cause. Sometimes we say things too quickly. Sometimes we wish we could take back things we have said in the heat of anger or from the depths of a bad mood. Sometimes our inexperience causes us to blurt out things we later realize we shouldn't have said.

In these particular verses, King Solomon is instructing his son on the best way to get out of a verbal contract. In our American culture, the use of credit (buying something now that you will pay for later) is widely accepted. Most people make major purchases by using a credit card and making payments over a period of time. In ancient Israel, however, borrowing was something done only in the most critical circumstances. In those times as well as today, whenever money is borrowed, a guarantee must be made, insuring that the borrower will pay back the lender. King Solomon told his son, "Look, don't ever say that you will pay for another person's debts! Don't get yourself into financial messes with your mouth!"

Financial messes aren't the only kind of problems we can get ourselves into with our mouths. There are a lot of things we can say that will end up "trapping" us. I had something happen to me just recently that proves the point.

Dig Site

Read Proverbs 6:1-5

Artifacts In Situ

- insurance papers
- telephone

Today's Treasure

Go and humble yourself; press your plea with your neighbor! Allow no sleep to your eyes, no slumber to your eyelids.
Proverbs 6:3b,4

When an older gentleman ran into my van last summer, I had to deal with his insurance company in order to be compensated for the damage he had caused. The company was very slow to help me, even though their client was the sole cause of the accident.

My family had been looking forward to a special trip for my son David's birthday. He was taking along a friend, and there would have been plenty of room for everyone to travel comfortably in our van (which was totaled in the wreck). However, there was not enough room for six people in the rental car the insurance company had provided us. The insurance people were not very nice, and they were not easy to work with. I was afraid that David's birthday was going to be ruined because we weren't going to be able to make the trip without a larger vehicle.

I called the company. Since the man I needed to talk with was not available, I left a message on his voice mail. I let him have it for the terrible service we had received from the company and for single-handedly ruining my son's birthday! When I was finished with my tirade, I hung up the phone.

I tried to go about my daily activities, but it wasn't very long before God began to convict me. That insurance guy didn't need me to vent my frustration on his voice mail. Who knows what kind of life he lived? Who knows what kind of pressure he was under? Were my actions going to do anything to point him to Christ? No, I'm afraid not.

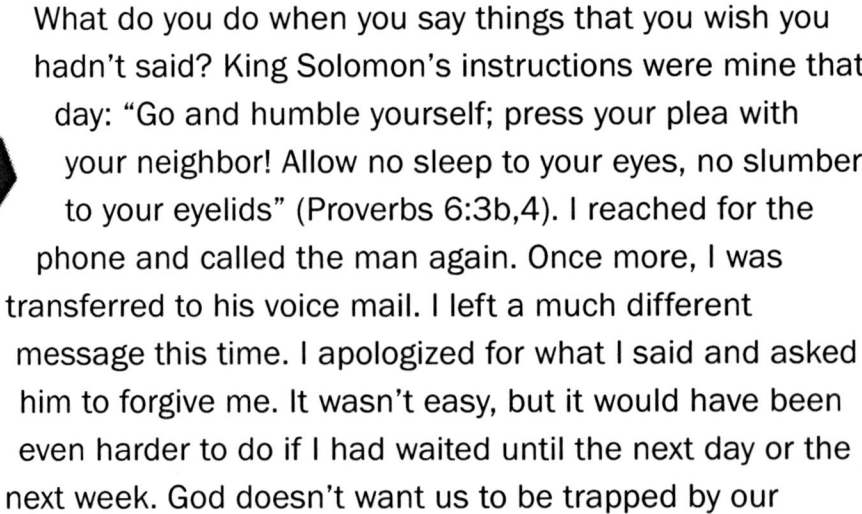

What do you do when you say things that you wish you hadn't said? King Solomon's instructions were mine that day: "Go and humble yourself; press your plea with your neighbor! Allow no sleep to your eyes, no slumber to your eyelids" (Proverbs 6:3b,4). I reached for the phone and called the man again. Once more, I was transferred to his voice mail. I left a much different message this time. I apologized for what I said and asked him to forgive me. It wasn't easy, but it would have been even harder to do if I had waited until the next day or the next week. God doesn't want us to be trapped by our words. If we find ourselves in a bind, the best thing to do is to apologize — immediately!

I received a phone call from the insurance man later that day. He said in all his years of working for that company, he had received many calls like the first message I left, but none like the second message. No one had ever apologized to him for being rude. He forgave me, and he told me that I had actually made his day!

When I was young, if I ever said something that I shouldn't, or took a "tone" with my parents, my mother would say to me, "You better take that back before it gets cold." We can talk our way into messes, but if we try hard enough, we can talk our way out of them, especially when we start with an apology. Jesus told His disciples, "Let me tell you something: Every one of these careless words is going to come back to haunt you. There will be a time of Reckoning. Words are powerful; take them seriously."[22]

Data Entry

🖉 Read James 3:1-12. Copy verse two here.

_____

_____

_____

🖉 What do you do when you say something you wish you hadn't?

_____

_____

_____

🖉 How do you treat people when they come to you with an apology?

_____

_____

_____

Unearthing the Treasures of Solomon's Proverbs

_____

_____

_____

_____

_____

✏ Work on your passage for memorization.

✏ What is today's date? _____ Take a few moments to journey to your Prayeramid.

Quotable

"Kind words do not cost much. They never blister the tongue or lips. They make other people good-natured. They also produce their own image on men's souls, and a beautiful image it is."
Blaise Pascal

Tuesday
Unit Six • Wisdom Stays Out of Trouble

Active Ants: High Hopes for the Greatest Generation

Dig Site

Read Proverbs 6:6-15

Artifacts In Situ

- can of bug spray

Today's Treasure

Go to the ant, you sluggard; consider its ways and be wise!
Proverbs 6:6

work ethic *The attitude of a group or a society toward work, especially the attitude or belief that work is good for man and higher on society's scale of values than play or leisure.*[23]

For eight years, my family lived in a wonderful house with only one problem. Ants showed up every spring. Not just one or two ants, but colonies of "sugar" ants (the tiny ones) claimed our home as theirs. When we were moving to Nashville and first went to look at this house, I noticed a few ants on the kitchen floor. At the time, I thought, *Oh, a little bug spray will get rid of those ants. No problem.* I didn't know, however, just how much of a problem they would be.

It turns out these pesky little creatures annoy archaeologists as well, especially fire ants (the big ones). An archaeologist working in the Southern United States noted, "The thing that struck me about fire ants is that you won't know that there are a dozen crawling up your leg until they all decided to sting you simultaneously." Oh, well, you've got to admire their team work!

Ants are hard workers. They have no rulers, but each colony of ants has three classes: the

---

Unearthing the Treasures of Solomon's Proverbs

queens, the workers, and the males. They provide food for themselves and their young. They have a strong work ethic.

Some people think that Americans have lost our *work ethic*. Americans today are not so concerned with great accomplishments as we once were. Over fifty years ago, at the conclusion of World War II, Americans came back from a hard-fought victory ready to make wonderful lives for themselves. This particular group of Americans has been labeled the "greatest generation" because they saw what could happen if they didn't work hard enough. With their own eyes, they saw countries ravaged by cruel dictators because people didn't fight hard enough for freedom. Unfortunately, today's generation of young adults has known only peace and prosperity, for the most part. In exchange for living pleasant lives, we've lost our motivation to make things better. We seem to be okay with things the way they are.

The truth is that things are not okay. Our country is on the edge of collapse because the forces of evil are not being reigned in through the prayers of God's people. Have Christians forgotten God's ways?

▲ The value of every human life is right. Abortion is wrong.

▲ Marriage as defined by Almighty God, a commitment made between one man and one woman, is right. Homosexuality, adultery, and fornication are wrong.

▲ Loving your neighbor is right. Racism is wrong.

▲ Maintaining a healthy lifestyle through proper nutrition and exercise is right. Drugs are wrong.

▲ Living for Christ is right. Living for yourself is wrong.

I've got high hopes for you and for your brothers and sisters. I personally believe that yours will be the greatest generation. Are you willing to confront the culture with God's truth? Just as an ant can move things that are double and triple his own size, we can move things in our world that are seemingly immovable through the power of the God of the Universe, who bends His ear to hear our prayers.

One of the reasons the ants in our old house were so hard to get rid of was because every spring a new generation of ants moved in. I would get rid of one set, then, *here came their babies!* They came even more quickly because they were using the ant superhighways that their parents had built. They didn't have to do as much work because a path had already been routed for them. Rather than become lazy, however, they used the time and energy they would have spent foraging new tunnels to provide for their families and to build their colonies.

Are your parents doing everything they can to lay the groundwork for you, to build the tunnels, pave the way, and provide the best roadmap available? If so, don't let that make you lazy in your faith. Let it spur you on to greater heights.

Data Entry

One of the favorite songs of the "greatest generation" was "High Hopes," by Sammy Cahn. Take a look at an excerpt from the lyrics:

Just what makes that little ol' ant

Think he'll move that rubber tree plant?

Anyone knows an ant can't

Move a rubber tree plant!

But he's got high hopes . . . he's got high hopes!

He's got high, apple pie in the sky hopes!

So any time you're getting low

'Stead of letting go,

Just remember that ant.

Oops! There goes another rubber tree plant.

What is the point of the song?

_____
_____
_____
_____

✎ How is the ant going to accomplish what he wants to do?

_____
_____

✎ What are some things you want to do that you can accomplish with hard work?

_____
_____
_____

✎ What are some things that can only be accomplished through prayer?

_____
_____
_____
_____

✎ Copy Matthew 19:26 here.

_____

_____

_____

_____

_____

_____

✎ What is today's date? _____ Take a few moments to journey to your Prayeramid.

Quotable

"Growing up in a boarding house introduced me to hard work and taught me the value of diligent labor. I learned to shuck corn, shell peas, wash dirty dishes, set the table, shop for my mother at the corner grocery store and even flip eggs and pancakes on the grill." S. Truett Cathy

Wednesday

Unit Six • Wisdom Stays Out of Trouble

Terrible Troublemakers: 7 UPs God Hates

There it is. Right there in the Word of God, Proverbs 6:16-19 lists seven things that God hates. This list deserves our serious consideration. To me, it is a very uncomfortable feeling to think that I could be doing something that God hates. I don't want that in my life! I want to be as far away from that as I can be. Let's take a look at what *not* to do.

Act UP. What the NIV translation calls "haughty eyes," other translations call a *proud look,*[24] *arrogant eyes,*[25] and *eyes of pride.*[26] There were some kids in my middle school who thought they were very cool — so much better than everyone else. They never said that's what they thought about themselves. They didn't have to. Their eyes told the whole story of the attitude in their hearts. God hates that.

Talk it UP. The second troublemaker on the list is a lying tongue. Why is it that Satan can so easily fool us into thinking that lying will solve our problems? It never, ever will. It only makes things worse. God hates that.

Frame UP. What could be more wicked than hands that shed innocent blood? Looking at the recorded accounts of the murder of our Lord Jesus, we find Pilate, the Roman governor, as the key decision-maker in the final verdict. Pilate

Dig Site

Read Proverbs 6:16-19

Artifacts In Situ

⚲ aluminum soft drink can

Today's Treasure

There are six things the Lord hates, seven that are detestable to him: . . .
Proverbs 6:16

didn't want to crucify Jesus. He knew Jesus had been framed. He couldn't find that Jesus had done anything wrong. Yet to save his political position of power, he let the people have their way and sentenced Jesus to crucifixion. Pilate's hands were guilty of shedding innocent blood, and he knew it. Matthew 27:24 tells us, "So [Pilate] sent for a bowl of water and washed his hands before the crowd, saying, 'I am innocent of the blood of this man. The responsibility is yours!'" I don't think he could get out of murder that easily, do you? God hates that.

Think UP. There really are people who sit around all day and think about doing terrible things. Sometimes people might be motivated by what they see on TV. Sometimes people are motivated by revenge, hate, or unforgiveness. There is so much good that could be done in this world. There are many worthwhile organizations that would love to have the time and energy that some people spend inventing evil things to do. A mind is a terrible thing to waste. God hates that.

Hurry UP. It seems that some people just want to get into trouble. They are actually in a hurry to be up to no good. Their feet rush them to parties and other places where they can hurt themselves and others. God is never in a hurry; have you noticed that?

Do you remember the story of the adulterous woman, found in John 8:3-11? This woman was caught committing adultery, and the religious leaders of the town brought her to Jesus. They were in a hurry to punish her and to trap Him. Was Jesus in a hurry? Not one bit. He told them that the one without sin could cast the first stone at the woman. Suddenly, no one was in a hurry. They weren't in a hurry to take an honest look at the evil in their own lives, just in a hurry to bring trouble on others. God hates that.

Make UP. It looks like God is mentioning lying twice in this passage. He is, but this second time is about "lying under oath." A person who lies under oath is lying when they have promised to tell the truth, and most likely, someone else's life or reputation is at stake. God hates that.

Stir UP. You know the kind of person who likes to get things stirred up. This is a person who tells one person something, gets a reaction, and then goes and tell someone else what happened. Stirring up trouble is something godly men should stay away from, and yet, it seems that gossip is nearly irresistible. Resist it! Friendships can break, churches can split, and peaceful neighbors can become bitter enemies when someone begins to stir up trouble. God hates that.

Data Entry

✎ Are you surprised by any of the things that God hates?

_____

_____

✎ Why do you think lying (although different forms of it) was mentioned twice?

_____

_____

✎ Are you guilty of any of these 7 UPs? Ask God, and record your thoughts here.

_____

_____

_____

_____

✎ What is today's date? _____ Take a few moments to journey to your Prayeramid.

Quotable

"Suppose someone should offer me a plateful of crumbs after I had eaten a T-bone steak. I would say, 'No, thank you. I am already satisfied.' Christian, that is the secret — you can be so filled with the things of Christ, so enamored with the things of God that you do not have time for the sinful pleasures of the world."
Billy Graham

Thursday
Unit Six • Wisdom Stays Out of Trouble

A Real Relationship: Show and Tell

Dig Site

Read Proverbs 6:20-35

Artifacts In Situ

- WWJD bracelet

Today's Treasure

Bind them upon your heart forever; fasten them around your neck.
Proverbs 6:21

A few years ago when my son David was four years old, he asked for a WWJD bracelet. They were popular at the time, and he had noticed several people at church wearing them. I thought it was a great idea. The sooner we learn to ask ourselves, "What would Jesus do?" the better!

We bought one at the Christian bookstore. I tried to explain to David, in words simple enough for a four-year-old, the concept behind WWJD. I was sure he understood because the rest of that afternoon and evening, David was an extremely good boy. He played nicely with his sister and brother and was obedient to his dad and me. The next morning, however, we had barely started the day when I heard cries coming from the living room. Danya, then 6 years old, was holding her stomach and crying, "He hit me!"

I began to comfort Danya and looked at David questioningly. "What did we talk about yesterday, son?" I asked. "Did you remember to ask yourself, *What would Jesus do?*"

"It's okay, Momma," he said in all innocence. "I'm not wearing my bracelet today."

Okay, he was four years old. What about the rest of us? What's our excuse? All too often people think they can live Christian lives that are inconsistent with Lordship.

What is Lordship? Lordship means that you have surrendered control of your life to Jesus Christ. He's in charge. You are following Him on purpose. It consumes your life — your thoughts, speech, and behavior. You see, being a Christian is not something you wear like a bracelet, putting it on when it's convenient. It is something you live even when you would rather be doing something else. When you would rather give way to a pity party, a temper tantrum, a critical comment, or a lustful leer, you pause to consider, *WWJD?* And you choose to submit to His Lordship.

I've seen Christian bumper stickers on cars carrying drivers who don't have any road manners at all. I've seen celebrities wearing cross necklaces but using their talents to promote themselves and their immoral lifestyles. And this hypocrisy is not limited to strangers in traffic or the Hollywood elite. It's a double standard that can hit close to home.

Is our Christianity just an outward display of religion? Or is Christianity a relationship that is driven to pursue an authentic submission to Jesus Christ as Lord? In spite of God's call to total obedience, many people who call themselves Christians lead lives very much like that of non-Christians.

I used to work with an Egyptian man named Khalil who was a devout Muslim. Everyone in the office respected Khalil for his strict adherence to his beliefs. They asked him lots of questions about it because he made it look fascinating. Khalil's beliefs made a difference in the way he lived. His actions stirred an interest in the hearts of other people. When I think about Khalil, I have to ask myself some hard questions. Why wasn't anyone in the office asking me about my religion? Why wasn't anyone interested in Christianity because of the way I lived?

In our nation of religious freedom, a cry for tolerance insists all roads lead to heaven. You may worship God, Allah, Buddha, the Goddess, the Supreme

Being — whatever. After all, it's all the same thing, right? No, it's not the same. The difference in Christianity and every other belief in the world must be found in the fact that we aren't practicing a religion about God, but we are pursuing a relationship with God. That doesn't come about by wearing bracelets. It comes about by constantly examining the heart.

Data Entry

🖉 What do others think about Christianity when they look at your life? Does it look appealing to them? Are they interested in learning more?

_____
_____
_____
_____
_____
_____
_____

🖉 Work on your passage for memorization.

🖉 What is today's date? _____ Take a few moments to journey to your Prayeramid.

Quotable

"The greatest challenge facing the church today is to reassert the Lordship of Christ." Chuck Colson

Unearthing the Treasures of Solomon's Proverbs

Friday — Unit Six • Wisdom Stays Out of Trouble

Lab Work: Artifacts and Heartifacts

⇨ Read back through Proverbs 6 and your data entries for this week.

⇨ Complete any unanswered questions from this week's lessons.

⇨ What will last from your study of Proverbs 6? List this week's Artifacts and Heartifacts below.

Artifacts	Heartifacts
_____	_____
_____	_____
_____	_____
_____	_____

⇨ Do some soul-searching about what God is teaching you. Record your thoughts below.

_____
_____
_____
_____

⇨ Work on your Scripture memory passage. You can do it!

⇨ Take a few moments to journey to your Prayeramid.

⇨ Don't forget this week's EXTRA! Ask a grandparent or an older person you know what "work ethic" means. Ask him or her how the work ethic of our country has changed (or if it has). Record this person's thoughts here.

| Preview | **Unit Seven • Written on Your Heart** |

Monday

Wisdom Remains on the Sidewalk: Listen to Your Mummy

Tuesday

Wisdom Reveals the Enemy: Taken by Surprise

Wednesday

Wisdom Retains His Innocence: "He Said, She Said"

Thursday

Wisdom Rests on a Firm Foundation: Christ, the Cornerstone

Friday

Lab Work: Artifacts and Heartifacts

This Week's EXTRA

Ask your mom out on a date this week. Make your plans with her fun in mind, and be sure to choose things she would like to do. Enjoy spending one-on-one time with your mom, and treat her to something special.

Monday

Unit Seven • Written on Your Heart

Wisdom Remains on the Sidewalk: Listen to Your Mummy

Dig Site

Read Proverbs 7:1-5

Artifacts In Situ

- scrapbooks
- photos
- minivans

Today's Treasure

Keep my commands and you will live; guard my teachings as the apple of your eye.
Proverbs 7:2

We moms probably demand a lot of the same things from our sons: *Put the lid down. Clean up your room. Give me a kiss.* And we probably pray a lot of the same things for our sons: *Give him a compassionate heart, Lord. Make him a servant of Your Kingdom. Direct his paths.*

As a mother, I can vouch for the fact that there's something about my relationships with each of my sons that has its own distinct flavor. Is it because each of my boys reminds me of their dad? Is it because in looks and gestures, they sometimes make me think of my own daddy? Or is it because for each of them, I know that I am the first woman they ever truly loved?

My friend Kyla recently showed me a scrapbook she was putting together for her son, Aaron. Aaron is a baseball player with his eyes on a college scholarship, and this scrapbook lovingly chronicled his Little League and high school career. Packed with pictures and newspaper clippings, Kyla has created a treasure of memories that Aaron can enjoy all his life. If he doesn't already know it, one day Aaron will realize that his mom is his biggest fan. All his dreams are her dreams, too.

Unearthing the Treasures of Solomon's Proverbs

We moms see promise in our sons for great things. And we see prospective problems, too. We see the hindrances that can come along and distract our boys from living up to their full potential — namely, girls! In the seventh chapter of Proverbs, King Solomon reminds his son to be diligent in keeping his teachings. He warns his son that lacking judgment when it comes to women can actually cost him his life. This is a strong teaching that, at first glance, may seem as though it doesn't apply to you. After all, it's not like you have any adulterous women chasing you. Read author and mom Lisa Whelchel's take on Proverbs 7. She wrote it for her son.

Proverbs 7[27]

1 My son, keep my words and if you value your life,

2 Keep my commands. My law is the law, don't ever forget it.

3 Tie a string around your finger or tattoo it on your heart.

4 Say to wisdom, "You are my sister" and call understanding, "Mom."

5 Listen to your mother and sister for they will keep you away from the girls.

6 For from my minivan I looked through the window,

7 And I saw a bunch of junior high boys
And one naïve young man, in particular.

8 Passing along the street near the mall;
And entering through Sears,

9 just after dark, before all the stores closed.

10 And there a girl met him,
Wearing a shirt that revealed her belly button (and her heart).

11 She laughed way too loudly. She was rarely at home with her parents.

12 She seemed to turn up everywhere, at the mall, the movies,
hanging out at friends' houses.

13 So she playfully hugged the young man and gave him a friendly kiss on the cheek.
With a spunky look she said to him,

14 "I just came from youth group and I played the part.

15 I was hoping to see you there and when I didn't see you I came looking for you. I'm so glad I found you.

16 I have fixed up my room really cool.

17 I bought a bunch of good smelling stuff from Bath & Body Works.

18 Why don't you come over and we can watch some videos and make out.

19 My parents aren't at home, they are away on a business trip.

20 They won't be back until Tuesday."

21 With her convincing innocence, he bought it.
All it took was, "I've never met a guy I can talk to like you before," and she had him.

22 He fell for it, hook, line, and sinker.

23 'Til he felt the hook in his mouth.
As a fish swimming for the worm,
He didn't know it was a trap until it was too late.

24 Now, listen up guys, and listen up good.
I know what I'm talking about:

25 Don't even look down that path.
If you don't want to end up where the road is headed
Then stay on the sidewalk.

26 Girls have been the fall of many a strong Christian young man.
They can lead you away from God and you could end up losing your life –
at least the abundant one God has planned for you.

Moms know. You've trusted your mom all these years. Trust her now. Ask her. Talk to her. Then listen to your mummy! Your mom is your key to understanding women.

Data Entry

🖉 Have you scheduled your date with your mom yet? Be prepared to enjoy a special evening. You may want to have a list of questions or things you would like to talk about with your mom. Find out some things you've always wanted to know:

> What was her most embarrassing teen moment?
> Who was her best friend?
> What was her greatest struggle as a teen?
> What were her dreams?
> How did she meet your dad?
> If your mom is a Christian, ask her how she met the Lord.

You may want to ask your mom to reveal her insight into your life.

> What does she see as your greatest strengths?
> Your weaknesses?
> Your gifts and talents?
> What are her greatest hopes for you?

🖉 The Scripture passage you chose should be fully memorized now. Recite it from memory to a parent this week.

🖉 What is today's date? _____ Check the appendix for your Password to Prayer.

Quotable

"Only God Himself fully appreciates the influence of a Christian mother in the molding of character in her children." Billy Graham

| Tuesday | Unit Seven • Written on Your Heart |

Wisdom Reveals the Enemy: Taken by Surprise

The ancient city of Pompeii in Italy lies under fair blue skies near the Mediterranean shore. Wealthy Romans flocked to Pompeii, building beautiful homes in this country area that offered all the conveniences of a city. The prosperous town was an industrial and trade center known for its specialties: fish sauce, perfume, and cloth. Daily life was routine for the families who lived there, enjoying the majestic view of Mount Vesuvius. They didn't know it was a volcano just waiting to erupt. In A.D. 63, it did.

The eruption caused some damage to Pompeii and a few surrounding cities. Statues toppled over, and some buildings suffered architectural damage. However, rather than take this as a sign that more volcanic activity could occur in the future, the people of Pompeii chose to repair their city and continue living there. They didn't believe they were in any danger. In fact, they appreciated the rich soil the lava had formed. Their plowing and planting were never better.

But sixteen years later, in the summer of A.D. 79, Mount Vesuvius awoke from its nap and violently spewed a torrent of lava from its wide mouth. Hot ashes, stones, and cinders fell from the sky upon the townspeople of Pompeii, who were taken by surprise. Many managed to escape, but there

Dig Site

Read Proverbs 7:6-12

Artifacts In Situ

- statues
- bricks
- columns

Today's Treasure

I saw among the simple, I noticed among the young men, a youth who lacked judgment.
Proverbs 7:7

Unearthing the Treasures of Solomon's Proverbs

were many victims as well, buried alive with the city under mounds of volcanic ash.

The city began to be excavated in the 1860's. Archaeologists discovered the layer of ash had actually done a great job of preserving the city — showing a town and a people living regular old life when the volcano erupted.

It is in our regular old life when the volcano of our inner man can often erupt, and we, along with those around us, are taken by surprise.

We say things we wish we hadn't when we are tired and aggravated.

We tease our siblings in front of their friends and instantly wish we could take it back.

We laugh behind someone's back and then feel bad all day.

When we give in to Satan's prompting, we have no one to blame but ourselves. The writer of the book of James put it this way: "Don't let anyone under pressure to give in to evil say, 'God is trying to trip me up.' God is impervious to [not influenced by] evil, and puts evil in no one's way. The temptation to give in to evil comes from us and only us. We have no one to blame but the leering, seducing flare-up of our own lust."[28]

In the Scripture you read today, this is exactly what's happening. The young man has put himself in the way of temptation. Like the townspeople of Pompeii who were living in the shadow of an active volcano, he is walking around in dangerous territory. If you go through the wrong places, instead of avoiding them, then you are going to encounter evil. It will be waiting for you. You have an enemy. Will you recognize him? Or will you be taken by surprise?

God says the devil is like a roaring lion.[29] Lions are really sneaky animals. They laze around for up to 21 hours a day, and then in the darkest, coolest hours of the early morning, they begin to hunt. A lion will target the weak, unsuspecting prey. Similarly, the devil will target the weak, unsuspecting Christian. The lion's chief tactic is in the element of surprise. He stalks his prey, rushing in for the kill at rivers or water holes, where animals let down their guards. The devil is the same way. Skilled in his tactics, he has infiltrated the places we think are safe. His greatest strategy is in making us believe he does not exist.

Data Entry

✏️ How would you define the word "enemy"? Use a dictionary or your own words to explain what this word means to you.

_____
_____
_____

✏️ Do you have any enemies?

_____
_____
_____

✏️ Imagine Satan has a filing cabinet. In your file, he keeps a record of the best ways to trip you up. What does he have down for you? List some of your weakest areas. (For example, what really makes you mad? What are the things that make you act ungodly?)

_____
_____
_____
_____
_____
_____

✏ Take a look at the answers you listed for the previous question. Write down some ideas for a more Christian response when these frustrating things happen. Pray for God to help you put this into action when you are next attacked!

_____

_____

_____

_____

_____

✏ The Scripture passage you chose should be fully memorized now. Recite it from memory to a parent this week.

✏ What is today's date? _____ Take a few moments to journey to your Prayeramid.

Quotable

"For more than 14 years I was the prey of the enemy. I thought I knew what was best for me. I wanted God only as my emergency Savior, when I was in a crisis and needed Him. And if you're like I was, the lion has you in his jaws." Dennis Rainey

| **Wednesday** | Unit Seven • Written on Your Heart |

Wisdom Retains His Innocence:
He Said, She Said

By Marilyn Morris[30]

Dig Site

Read Proverbs 7:13-23

Artifacts In Situ

- party clothes
- basketball

Today's Treasure

All at once he followed her . . . little knowing it will cost him his life.
Proverbs 7:22a, 23b

It was the last week in March, two months before graduation and the night air was cool. Kevin left the party at 11:30 and had only driven a block when he saw Jessica walking alone down the street. He stopped his car and asked if she wanted a ride home. She jumped in the car without hesitation, but they didn't go anywhere. At first they just talked. Then one thing led to another. The next thing Kevin knew they were having sex. Kevin then drove around the corner, dropped Jessica off in front of her house, and went home. . . Or at least that's the story Kevin told the police. The story Jessica told was very different.

According to Jessica, she left the party around 11:30 and started her short walk home when Kevin pulled up beside her and offered to take her home. The night air was cool and she took him up on the offer without hesitation. When she got in the car, she said he forced himself on her and raped her. The attorney telling the story said Kevin escaped going to prison for only one reason — his parents had the money to pay for a really good attorney. Without paying the $125,000 for a top notch attorney, Kevin might be sitting in prison today. The attorney went on to say this cat and mouse game of "He Said, She Said" goes on all the time.

So who was the innocent victim in this story? Was it Jessica? Did Kevin actually force her to have sex that evening? Will she be dealing with devastating memories that will haunt her for the rest of her life? Or was Kevin the innocent victim? Did Jessica make up the entire story while destroying Kevin's reputation, not to mention costing Kevin's parents over $100,000? No one but Kevin and Jessica will ever know the truth about what transpired that night because there were no other witnesses.

Now consider the rape case against basketball star Kobe Bryant.

Kobe was on top of the world. In 1996 he went from playing basketball in high school directly into the pros and had an impressive rookie season with the LA Lakers. The following year he became the youngest All-Star in NBA history. His wholesome image as an athlete, husband, and father provided multimillion-dollar endorsements. It was as if nothing could bring Kobe Bryant down. That is until June 30, 2003, when he opened the door and invited a 19-year-old girl into his hotel room in Colorado. A few hours later the cat and mouse game of "He Said, She Said" was set into motion, and Kobe Bryant's life changed forever when he was charged with sexually assaulting the 19-year-old girl.

Kobe and Kevin seem to have a great deal in common. Both are in the prime of their lives. No doubt both felt somewhat invincible. Kobe was looking forward to yet another successful year with the NBA making millions of dollars while Kevin was looking forward to graduation and then heading off to college. Both men have been charged with rape. And while we may never know if Kobe and Kevin are innocent or guilty, we do know one thing for certain about them. Had they chosen sexual abstinence (purity) until marriage and faithfulness inside marriage, neither would have gone through the nightmare and public humiliation they now face.

Abstinence would have provided 100 percent protection for Kobe and Kevin as well as 100 percent protection for their families. Kobe would simply be known as one of America's top basketball superstars, and Kevin would be just another cute freshman guy on a college campus. But now because of one brief moment in history, people will always remember them as two more guys who have been accused of rape.

Data Entry

🖉 Eventually, Jessica dropped the charges against Kevin, and Kobe Bryant's accuser dropped the charges against him. The consequences of these events, however, will be felt for years. Take some time to consider how Kevin's fornication (pre-marital sex) will affect his future wife. Record your thoughts below.

_____
_____
_____
_____
_____

🖉 Think about how Kobe's adultery has affected his wife and family.

_____
_____
_____
_____

🖉 How can you best avoid a "He Said, She Said" situation?

_____
_____
_____
_____

Unearthing the Treasures of Solomon's Proverbs

🖉 The Scripture passage you chose should be fully memorized now. Recite it from memory to a parent this week.

🖉 What is today's date? _____ Take a few moments to journey to your Prayeramid.

Quotable

"Sure, you can learn from making mistakes. But the emphasis in Scripture is on being obedient to God in the first place. Proverbs tells us to listen to what wisdom has to say, listen to the pain that you can avoid if you do the right thing." Joshua Harris

Thursday

Unit Seven • Written on Your Heart

Wisdom Rests on a Firm Foundation: Christ, the Cornerstone

Faith•quake (fAth'kwAk) n. a shaking or trembling of one's faith caused by extreme tragedy or disaster and producing an upheaval which leads to radical change

In July, 1986, Doug and Evon Herman were in love with each other and with the Lord. The young couple were the proud parents of their toddler son, Joshua Ryan. Doug was pursuing a degree from Bible college while employed as a full-time youth pastor. Sweethearts since their high school days and married just after Evon graduated, the Hermans were eagerly serving the Lord together in ministry. Bright, energetic, and upbeat, they looked forward to passing on their heritage of faith to a family they hoped would include several more children.

Their hopes were destroyed when Evon's gynecologist summoned the young family to his office. Eighteen months earlier, just after delivering Josh, Evon had required a blood transfusion. The doctor informed them that one of the two units of blood given to Evon at that time had been infected with the HIV virus (the virus that causes AIDS). The Hermans' young lives were devastated as the doctor explained that now tests showed that Evon was infected with HIV as well.

Dig Site

Read Proverbs 7:24-27

Artifacts In Situ

- Bible
- blood test

Today's Treasure

Many are the victims she has brought down; her slain are a mighty throng. Her house is a highway to the grave, leading down to the chambers of death.
Proverbs 7:26,27

Unearthing the Treasures of Solomon's Proverbs

Doug, who grew up in a Christian home, explains, "I had learned that if you serve God and if you live right, He will bless you. If you serve God and if you live right, He will protect you. But that was not what was happening in my life."

Many times, Christians believe that if they do everything right, God will keep His hand of blessing on them. "The reality is that it might not happen," states Doug. "When tragedy occurs — when somebody's spouse leaves them, when an earthquake or a disaster falls, when we lose loved ones, or when we lose our physical ability because of cancer or Crohn's disease, we think, 'God, where are you? What did You do?' Our faith is so tied to our temporal, physical experiences that we can't get past those faithquake experiences to find out that our faith still is intact, regardless of what happens."

After going through the tragedy of losing his wife and also a baby daughter, Doug readily admits there is a difference in where he is now, spiritually, and where his faith was during those trials. "My faith today is not based on what God does or does not do for me. Whether God gives me all the blessings of the world or if my life is full of tragedies, my faith must be based on Who He is. He's still my God, and I'll serve Him regardless. Before, my faith was based in the promises, not in the One Who makes the promises."

Doug went from one spiritual point to the other by asking God the difficult questions that were coursing through his mind and heart. "If you're going to question God," he advises, "then don't stop until you find an answer. Start digging — but don't stop until you hit something solid, like the cornerstone of your faith: Christ."

As Doug turned to his Bible for answers, he found several folks who had faithquakes of their own. One was John the Baptist.

John the Baptist was Jesus' blood relative. He knew Christ. Yet John found himself in a dungeon, about to be killed by the wicked Herod, even though he knew he had done nothing to deserve such a punishment. John knew Jesus was God, but Christ was not doing what John thought He would do.

Confused, John sent two of his disciples to ask Jesus if He was indeed the Messiah or if they should be looking for someone else.

Doug explains, "Jesus sent word to John assuring him that yes, He was the Messiah. Jesus also told the messengers to tell John, basically, 'Blessed is he who does not stumble on account of me. Blessed is he whose faith does not falter, who doesn't go through a faithquake because I'm not doing what he wants Me to do.'"[31]

"You have to realize that God will do what He wants to do. We must still trust Him, even when things fall apart — even if we're about to get beheaded! If we continue to believe in Him and trust Him, then we are highly blessed."

God wants you to know Him. He wants you to rely on Him and trust in Him, resting on the foundation of Christ as the cornerstone of your life. Trust Him through the good times and the bad times. You will be highly blessed.

Data Entry

AIDS stands for Acquired Immunodeficiency Syndrome. This disease renders the body unable to fight off the many infectious diseases it normally could if it were healthy. When the first cases of the disease were reported back in the 1980's, doctors and other healthcare workers didn't understand how it was spread. (Now we know that AIDS is spread mostly through sexual contact.) Unfortunately, the HIV virus contaminated portions of the nation's blood supply before anyone knew the damage it could cause. Our blood supply is safe today because all donated blood is tested for AIDS. Evon Herman was a victim of AIDS due to circumstances that were far beyond her control. What is the number one thing you can do to avoid the HIV virus?

_____

_____

_____

Unearthing the Treasures of Solomon's Proverbs

✏️ Have you experienced tragedy in your life? How can God use difficult times to draw us close to Him?

_____
_____
_____
_____
_____
_____

✏️ Are you ever tempted to think that if you are a good person, God owes you something? Do you get upset when things go well for a person who is not godly? Look up Matthew 5:45. What is Jesus saying?

_____
_____
_____
_____

✏️ The Scripture passage you chose should be fully memorized now. Recite it from memory to a parent this week.

✏️ What is today's date? _____ Take a few moments to journey to your Prayeramid.

Quotable

"We presume that it's our right to have health. It's our right to be successful. It's our right, because we are children of the King, to have victory, including physical well-being, a lack of pain, and a lack of suffering. [But] faith in God and becoming a child of the King means that we have citizenship in His Kingdom. It doesn't mean that our lives are going to be perfect." Doug Herman

Friday
Unit Seven • Written on Your Heart

Lab Work: Artifacts and Heartifacts

➪ Read back through Proverbs 7 and your data entries for this week.

➪ Complete any unanswered questions from this week's lessons.

➪ What will last from your study of Proverbs 7? List this week's Artifacts and Heartifacts below.

Artifacts	**Heartifacts**
_____	_____
_____	_____
_____	_____
_____	_____

➪ Do some soul-searching about what God is teaching you. Record your thoughts below.

_____

_____

_____

_____

➪ Work on your Scripture memory passage. You can do it!

➪ Take a few moments to journey to your Prayeramid.

➪ Don't forget this week's EXTRA! Ask your mom out on a date this week. Make your plans with her fun in mind, and be sure to choose things she would like to do. Enjoy spending one-on-one time with your mom, and treat her to something special.

Unearthing the Treasures of Solomon's Proverbs

Preview

Unit Eight • Wisdom's Invitation

Monday

Where: A Busy Intersection

Tuesday

When: A Daily Date

Wednesday

Who: Someone Like You

Thursday

RSVP: The Courtesy of a Reply is Requested

Friday

Lab Work: Artifacts and Heartifacts

This Week's EXTRA

Read the book of Ecclesiastes in a modern version. (You have this week and next week to complete this EXTRA.)

Monday

Unit Eight • Wisdom's Invitation

Where: A Busy Intersection

The entire book of Proverbs is an invitation — a cry — beckoning the reader to come to wisdom. In fact, Eugene Peterson, author of the paraphrase "The Message," translates Solomon's words in this way: *Wisdom **cries out** from the busiest intersection in town.*

Dig Site

Read Proverbs 8:1-11

Artifacts In Situ

- taxi cab
- lights
- shoes

Today's Treasure

Choose my instruction instead of silver, knowledge rather than choice gold, for wisdom is more precious than rubies, and nothing you desire can compare with her.
Proverbs 8:10,11

When I visited New York City, I saw firsthand the busiest intersection in the country: Times Square. I had never seen anything like it in my life. They call New York "the city that never sleeps" because the lights never go out on Times Square. You can walk outside anytime of the night, and Times Square is as bright as day because of all the lights — the streetlights, the brilliant glow from the posh hotels, the lights from the zillions of billboards that are all over the place, and even the beams from the headlights of the cars and taxis that creep along the crowded streets.

Times Square is noisy. Horns are honking constantly. Vendors market their wares with loud voices. Music blares from the shops. Television networks have huge screens facing the square, proclaiming the latest news, sports scores, and stock market numbers. And the people! The people have a sound all their own. Their feet are clomping, clipping, and clanking down the sidewalk. Humans of all languages — all colors,

---

Unearthing the Treasures of Solomon's Proverbs

shapes, and sizes — collide on these streets where the world crosses paths. It's Times Square, the busiest intersection in town.

My husband and I, along with two friends, rode through these streets in a genuine New York City taxi. I braced myself for an exciting ride. I had heard all about the crazy cab drivers! Our driver competently raced down the street, whipping in and out between cars and back and forth between lanes. Then, quite unexpectedly, he slammed on his brakes. Up ahead, I could make out the shadowy figure of a man waving his arms, imploring us to stop. He was standing in the middle of the road, just as we were approaching Times Square.

Frankly, I was a bit scared. After all, I've seen enough TV shows to know New York City is dangerous. I thought we were going to hit the man. Then, I thought the guy could be flagging us down in order to rob us or carjack the cab! All sorts of crazy scenarios raced through my mind.

As our flustered cabbie came to a screeching halt just inches from this young man, the guy began to sing. Yes, he sang! Taking advantage of the cab's headlights as though he were under the spotlight in a Broadway play, he began to perform. He stood in front of a taxi full of heart-pounding, breathless, frightened tourists, and he sang at the top of his lungs, "I LOVE NEW YORK!" Obviously drunk, the young man finished his concert with a grand flourish, bowed deeply for his captive audience, and our driver put the taxi in gear and sped around him.

This guy certainly got our attention. And what was his message? He loves New York. Big deal. This drunk punk stood in the way of a racing cab to deliver a worthless message. He put his life, as well as ours, in jeopardy to declare his love for a city — a love that expressed itself in getting drunk, partying, and acting stupidly.

Did I care that he loved New York? No. He didn't really love the city's lives; he merely loved the city life. Big difference.

Was his message important? No, not at all.

What does his love for New York mean to me? Nothing.

Does it make a difference in my life? Absolutely not.

But what if this had been his message:

> "You - I'm talking to all of you, everyone out here on the streets . . . Don't miss a word of this - I'm telling you how to live well, I'm telling you how to live at your best . . . Prefer my life-disciplines over chasing after money, and God-knowledge over a lucrative career. For Wisdom is better than all the trappings of wealth; nothing you could wish for holds a candle to her."[32]

Now, there's a message worth laying down one's life for. It's important. That message needs to stop traffic! It's God's message to all people.

Data Entry

🖉 Why is it so difficult for the voice of wisdom to be heard at a busy intersection?

_____

_____

_____

🖉 What are some foolish things that cry out for your attention? How can you quiet those cries in order to listen for Wisdom's Invitation?

_____

_____

_____

_____

🖉 Did you select a new Scripture to memorize? Write the reference here.

_____

Unearthing the Treasures of Solomon's Proverbs

🖉 Draw a picture of Lady Wisdom standing in the middle of a busy intersection, proclaiming the truth of God's Word. What would this look like to you? Spend some time on this. You're the only person who ever has to see it. Think about it: Draw it!

🖉 What is today's date? _____ Take a few moments to journey to your Prayeramid.

Quotable

"The glory of God, and, as our only means to glorifying Him, the salvation of human souls, is the real business of life." C. S. Lewis

Tuesday

Unit Eight • Wisdom's Invitation

When: A Daily Date

Dig Site

Read Proverbs 8:12-21

Artifacts In Situ

- clock radio
- cell phone
- gun

Today's Treasure

I love those who love me, and those who seek me find me.
Proverbs 8:17

My friend Lynnae and her husband Rob had been sleeping soundly one night when they were suddenly awakened by a banging sound. *Thump! Thump! Thump!* Drowsily, Lynnae looked around the dark bedroom. Immediately, she noticed the lights on her clock radio were not on. *"Oh,"* Lynnae thought, as she began to put the pieces together. *"It must be storming. The electricity has gone out. That thumping sound is the door of the shed in the backyard. It never stays closed! Rob should fix that. It bangs with the wind every time there's a storm . . . "* With everything settled in her mind, Lynnae began to drift back to sleep.

Suddenly, she heard the loud voice of a man yelling, "LET ME IN! LET ME IN!" Her eyes were wide open as she sat up in bed and fear gripped her heart. She could make out the shadowy image of Rob standing beside the window.

"They've cut off the power," he said. "Call the police — NOW!" From the bedroom window, Rob saw that someone had tampered with their utility box. He realized the thumping sound was a person banging on the back door, trying to break into their home. With no weapon of any kind in the house, Rob dashed to the back door, determined to somehow protect his wife and property.

Unearthing the Treasures of Solomon's Proverbs

"They? Who's they?" Lynnae wanted to scream as she searched frantically to find her cell phone in the dark house. Finally, she located it and was able to place a call to 911. Meanwhile, Rob began pounding on his side of the back door, screaming at the potential attacker on the other side. He got as violent and as loud as he could from his side of the door until the police arrived a few minutes later and the would-be thief ran off.

A few days later, Lynnae said, "I never went to sleep that night thinking our home would be attacked. We live in a safe neighborhood. We have close neighbors on all sides. We even live across the street from our church, where a security guard is on duty every night."

In the Bible, God warns us that our enemy, Satan, is like a thief. He attacks us when we least expect it. Does a thief call and warn you that he is going to rob you? Of course not. Likewise, Satan doesn't call ahead and say, "Hey — I'm going to tempt you at four o'clock today. Be ready."

But our Lord has told us that we *will* be tempted. We would be wise to be prepared for it. How do you prepare?

Preparation is a daily thing. Just as you get up and get dressed every day, you must wake up your spirit and get it dressed as well. Having a daily quiet time, a daily date with God, is essential to being prepared for whatever the day brings. There is, however, a problem: Because your daily date is the point at which your faith is strengthened, and it's where you learn to truly know and love God, it's the area where Satan will do his best to trip you up. If he can keep you from meeting with God, he can keep you from the benefits of God's love and wisdom in your life.

The best way to prepare for those unexpected attacks is to establish a battle plan. Meet with God every day. Read your Bible. Pray. Write in your journal. Or just sit still and think about Him. Take a few minutes each morning to tell the Lord you love Him. Thank Him for salvation. Thank Him for how wonderful it is to be growing up. Celebrate the Lord's favor and His hand of love on your life!

When Lynnae and Rob went to bed the night following the attack, things were different. This time, they were prepared for the unexpected. Each of them had a flashlight and a cell phone on their bedside tables. Outside, their utility box had been repaired and fitted with a padlock. A new gun was stowed underneath their bed, licensed and loaded.

Because they were prepared, they slept soundly. Nothing happened that night, or the next, or the next. But two weeks later, the same guy, the thief, returned. He pounded on the back door, screaming his head off. "LET ME IN!" he thundered. "LET ME IN!"

Lynnae immediately snatched her cell phone off the night table and dialed 911. Rob grabbed the new gun and ran toward the back door. Through the door, Rob screamed back at him, "What is your name? Who are you?"

"My name is Nathan!"

"I don't know you!" Rob cried, cocking the gun. At once, the thief ran off. He was just a bully! He had no weapons that could be used against my friends. He made a lot of noise and caused a lot of fear — but in the end, he ran away. Your enemy will run away, too, when you live a life that is daily prepared for his unexpected attacks.

Data Entry

🖉 Write down three reasons for having a daily date with God.

_____
_____
_____

🖉 Why do you think Rob wanted to know the man's name?

_____
_____
_____
_____

✏ As Christians, when we get comfortable spiritually, we are prone to attack. What kinds of things are going on in your life when the enemy is most likely to attack you?

_____

_____

_____

✏ Work on your passage for memorization.

✏ What is today's date? _____ Take a few moments to journey to your Prayeramid.

Quotable

"Well, for me, writing in my journal and singing songs to God are my two most effective ways to communicate with God. I almost don't have a relationship with God if I don't journal and I don't sing. They're my life force of relationship with God." Lamont Hiebert

Wednesday

Unit Eight • Wisdom's Invitation

Who: Someone Like You

Of all twelve disciples, I feel a real connection with Peter. Perhaps it's because Peter is portrayed so realistically throughout Scripture. From the New Testament, we can learn:

▲ Peter was opinionated and passionate,

▲ he was a big talker,

▲ he often spoke out of turn and could be argumentative--even with Jesus!--

▲ at times he was hot-tempered and impulsive, and

▲ Peter failed. He failed miserably.

Peter was just an ordinary fisherman living a normal life. Yet when Christ invited Peter to follow Him,[33] he left his fishing net and followed the Lord without hesitation. Along the way, Peter stumbled many times; he dragged his feet, he tripped up, and sometimes he got ahead of the Lord. But that's what I love most about Peter. I love his humanness, his imperfection. I find great comfort in the fact that someone so close to the Lord, someone who had lived with Him day after day for three years, someone who really loved God with all of his heart—someone like that could still fail. Someone like that could still be forgiven.

Dig Site

Read Proverbs 8:22-29

Artifacts In Situ

⚲ fishing net

Today's Treasure

I was appointed from eternity, from the beginning, before the world began.
Proverbs 8:23

Unearthing the Treasures of Solomon's Proverbs

It was on the night before the Crucifixion that Peter suffered through his greatest failure. After Jesus and the disciples had eaten the Passover meal, Christ tried to prepare them for what would happen that weekend. Jesus explained to these guys that every one of them would desert Him.[34] Good ol' Peter was so certain of his love for Christ that he declared, "Even if everyone else deserts You, I never will."[35] Can you see him, wide-eyed, chest out, looking down his long Jewish nose at the other guys? It was a prideful thing to say, but Peter sincerely couldn't see himself deserting his Lord. "Peter," Jesus replied, "the truth is, this very night, before the rooster crows, you will deny me three times."[36] Jesus knew that despite Peter's good intentions, he would fail Him.

Once Jesus was arrested, Peter secretly followed as the soldiers took Him to Caiaphas. He slipped into the courtyard where he could watch what was happening. A couple of people recognized him as one of the disciples, and both times, Peter angrily denied it. The book of Luke describes Peter's third and final denial this way:

> About an hour later another asserted, "Certainly this fellow was with him, for he is a Galilean."
>
> Peter replied, "Man, I don't know what you're talking about!" Just as he was speaking, the rooster crowed. The Lord turned and looked straight at Peter. Then Peter remembered the word the Lord had spoken to him....[37]

Has the Lord ever confronted you with the depth of your sin? Have you ever experienced that watershed moment, as Peter did, when the Lord looked you in the eye—caught your glance and held your gaze—and you crumbled, like Peter, under the weight of your conviction? Peter ran from the courtyard, sobbing bitterly, because he knew he had sinned.

Fortunately, Peter's story doesn't end with a broken man sobbing in the middle of the night on the back streets of Jerusalem. Jesus forgave Peter, and Peter was redeemed. He accepted Christ's forgiveness and walked in it with his head held high. He didn't dwell on the past and live a life of regret. No, eventually Peter got up, dried his eyes, blew his nose, and continued following Christ. In fact, fifty days after that terrible night of denial, Peter preached at Pentecost. His powerful sermon led three thousand people to faith in the risen Lord. It was another watershed moment—the beginning of the global spread of the Gospel and the start of the first church—and it happened to someone like Peter!

Like Peter, we have all failed. Despite many good intentions, we have all denied Christ at some point or another, and God knew that we would. In His great wisdom, He offered a plan of restoration through the death and resurrection of His Son. Peter's story reminds us that Christ offers forgiveness, redemption, and a wonderful new beginning. From the fisherman, like Peter, to the king, like Solomon, salvation in Christ is available for everyone—even someone like you!

Data Entry

Have you made a decision for Christ? In a couple of paragraphs, write down the story of the day you accepted Christ. In what ways has it affected your life? What was your life like before this decision? What is your life like now? In what ways do you want your life to serve Christ?

_____

_____

_____

_____

_____

_____

_____

_____

_____

_____

🖉 Perhaps you've never made Jesus the Lord of your life. Have you ever prayed and asked Christ to forgive you of your sins? Have you ever truly answered the invitation He has offered you? I invite you to pray this prayer and commit your life to Him today. He has a wonderful plan for you. Just pray: *Father, I am a sinner. I've done lots of wrong things in my life. I need a Savior. I need Your Son, Jesus. I want Him to be the Lord of my life. I accept the forgiveness His death bought for me, and I commit today to follow Him with my whole heart. In Jesus' Name, Amen.* If you prayed this prayer for the first time today, sign and date the line below, and share the wonderful news with your parents!

_____

🖉 Work on your passage for memorization.

🖉 What is today's date? _____ Take a few moments to journey to your Prayeramid.

Quotable

"In 1934, I made the decision to follow Christ. And I've never changed my mind. Though I have failed God many times, He has never failed me." Billy Graham

Thursday

Unit Eight • Wisdom's Invitation

R.S.V.P.: The Courtesy of a Reply is Requested

Dig Site

Read Proverbs 8:30-36

Artifacts In Situ

⚲ invitation

Today's Treasure

Blessed is the man who listens to me, watching daily at my doors, waiting at my doorway.
Proverbs 8:34

Have you noticed that life is full of invitations? You have received lots of invitations. From the time you were a baby, you were invited to friends' homes, to your grandparents' house, and to church. As you got older, you received invitations to birthday parties, the circus, and the movies. As a teenager, you'll find that invitations can be divided into three groups:

Invitations that Refresh. Anytime you are invited somewhere that makes you feel comfortable, it's refreshing. For instance, you may be invited to spend the night at a friend's house. While you are there, you and your friend spend time doing the things you love to do. You go fishing or shoot hoops. You eat pizza and your favorite snack foods. You stay up late playing video games. It's an invitation to fun!

Invitations that Stretch. Have you ever taken a rubber band and stretched it? I've received invitations that made me feel that way, stretched out of my comfort zone. Rich invited me to my first minor league ballgame after we were engaged. (This was long before I had children and turned into a baseball mom.) I had never been so bored in my life. I amused myself by trying out all the offerings at the concession stand. One inning

Unearthing the Treasures of Solomon's Proverbs

I had popcorn, then a hotdog, then nachos. Finally, at the end of the seventh inning, everyone stood up. I thought we were ready to leave — but it was only the "seventh inning stretch!" I had two more innings to go, and a stomach too full to eat anything else. I was stretched to the max.

Invitations that disappoint. Maybe you've been invited to a party and the host ignored you the entire time you were there. Or perhaps you've been invited to a church where no one welcomed you. Have you ever been invited on an outing with a couple of other friends and felt like a third wheel? When things don't go the way we expect them to, we are often disappointed.

The interesting thing about invitations is that they all come with an R.S.V.P. — the American abbreviation for the French phrase, "répondez s'il vous plaît." The English translation is: *The courtesy of a reply is requested.* In other words, what are you going to do with the invitation you have received? Will you accept the invitation or will you reject it?

Take a look at the picture you drew Tuesday. At every point of decision in your life, wisdom will be as obvious as a beautiful woman standing in the middle of a busy intersection, waving her arms and screaming for you to accept her invitation. Does she look out of place in the picture you drew? Wisdom doesn't exactly fit in with the American landscape of a bustling, chaotic city. But you notice her, don't you? You can't help it. The question is, when people who are so busy and moving so quickly through this life meet up with Wisdom, are they going to slow down? Are they going to stop and listen to Wisdom's invitation? And what will you do, young man, when you stand at a crossroads of your own?

You may find yourself at one of life's intersections even today. Every intersection is an invitation to making wise choices. So, R.S.V.P.!

When someone invites you to drink or smoke, Wisdom will be there. When someone tells you, "One time won't hurt anything," you will hear Wisdom's voice. When someone tries to show you a pornographic magazine or DVD, Wisdom's cry will rise above all the street noise: the hum of the crowd, the whiz of the vehicles, the beeping horns, and the music blaring from radios and storefronts. In reality, it is the still, small voice of a loving Father who knows what is best for you. If Jesus Christ is alive in you, that still small voice will be as vivid as a beautiful woman standing on top of a yellow taxi, waving her arms in the middle of Times Square.

Wisdom's invitation will take you to a place of deep refreshment. Will it stretch you? Absolutely. Will it disappoint you? Never. After studying Proverbs 8 this week, you have received Wisdom's invitation. Now, the courtesy of a reply is requested.

Data Entry

🖉 Copy this sentence: Every intersection is an invitation to making wise choices.

_____

_____

🖉 Have you ever received an invitation that ended up being disappointing? What happened?

_____

_____

_____

_____

🖉 How is Wisdom's invitation different? In what specific ways will it refresh and stretch you? List three.

_____

_____

_____

_____

🖉 Work on your passage for memorization.

🖉 What is today's date? _____ Take a few moments to journey to your Prayeramid.

Quotable

"If Jesus hears the faintest invitation of faith behind an unopened door, will He help open that door to save His sin-weakened child within? Hope eternal is that He will destroy the door and all else that separates us by keeping His steady hand on its latch." Stephen S. Sawyer

Friday
Unit Eight • Wisdom's Invitation

Lab Work: Artifacts and Heartifacts

⇨ Read back through Proverbs 8 and your data entries for this week.

⇨ Complete any unanswered questions from this week's lessons.

⇨ What will last from your study of Proverbs 8? List this week's Artifacts and Heartifacts below.

Artifacts	**Heartifacts**
_____	_____
_____	_____
_____	_____
_____	_____

⇨ Do some soul-searching about what God is teaching you. Record your thoughts below.

_____
_____
_____
_____
_____

⇨ Work on your Scripture memory passage. You can do it!

⇨ Take a few moments to journey to your Prayeramid.

⇨ Don't forget this week's EXTRA! Make time this week and next week to read through the book of Ecclesiastes in a Bible translation or paraphrase of your choice.

Unearthing the Treasures of Solomon's Proverbs

| Preview | **Unit Nine • Wisdom Sets a Table** |

Monday

The Menu: A Myriad of Choices

Tuesday

The House Specialty: A Teachable Spirit

Wednesday

The Main Course: Cleaning Your Plate

Thursday

The Table Scraps: Leftovers

Friday

Lab Work: Artifacts and Heartifacts

This Week's EXTRA

Complete your reading of Ecclesiastes.

Monday

Unit Nine • Wisdom Sets a Table

The Menu: A Myriad of Choices

When I was growing up, we had church-wide fellowship meals quite often. I looked forward to those times when our church family ate together. It was so much fun! Since I grew up without any grandparents, aunts, uncles, or cousins living close by, these experiences were like a large family gathering.

The meals were never catered by a restaurant. Instead, the ladies of the church always cooked their favorite dishes and brought them to our fellowship hall in the basement of the church. The delicious aromas wafted upstairs during the worship service. I wriggled and fidgeted in my hard pew seat until I'm sure my mother thought she would have to sit on me to keep me still. As soon as the last *amen* was said, I raced from the sanctuary to the basement. Somehow I always managed to maneuver my way through the crowd and make it to the front of the line. That's so funny to me, when I look back on it, because I was such a picky eater. I don't know what I was expecting to find.

I can remember standing at the head of what seemed like an endless table spread before me, covered in crisp white tablecloths and piled high with huge amounts of food. I traipsed through the line, eyeballing the typical Southern fare: dressed

Dig Site

Read Proverbs 9:1-6

Artifacts In Situ

- chicken bones
- French textbook
- Babylonian literature

Today's Treasure

Wisdom has built her house; she has hewn out its seven pillars.
Proverbs 9:1

Unearthing the Treasures of Solomon's Proverbs

eggs, baked beans, green beans, gelatin salads, cole slaw, and mashed potatoes. People would always laugh upon seeing my plate when I made it to the end of that smorgasbord. From a table heaped with choices, I took a roll and a chicken leg. And that's it.

The Bible tells the story of a young man who also stood at the head of a banquet table heaped high with food (and he was a picky eater, too). Daniel was a young Jew who was taken into captivity when Babylon attacked Jerusalem. The Babylonian king at that time, Nebuchadnezzar, was quite a military strategist. Besides taking down the king and looting the temple of God, Nebuchadnezzar took his line of attack one step further. He sent the head of his staff, Ashpenaz, to take as war prisoners the best and the brightest young men from the best and the brightest families. These boys would become an integral part of Babylon's future.

"Select only strong, healthy, and good-looking young men," [Nebuchadnezzar] said. "Make sure they are well versed in every branch of learning, are gifted with knowledge and good sense, and have the poise needed to serve in the royal palace. Teach these young men the language and literature of the Babylonians."[38] If the king could successfully immerse these young Hebrew men into the Babylonian culture, their language and their literature, he could make them Babylonians.

As a college student, I studied French. I was never very good at actually speaking the language, but I was a decent translator when it came to reading and writing it. Before my final exam, I spent the entire day at the library, studying every chapter in my book. I wrote down every vocabulary word, re-did the exercises, and read until my eyes were bloodshot. Walking home from the library that day, I realized that I was thinking in *French*. It was a great moment! I was so into it, so totally absorbed by my review, that my brain was translating my thoughts into French, automatically! It didn't last. I made an "A" on my test, but today, nearly twenty years later, I remember only a handful of French words and a few phrases. I am not a Frenchman! I am an English-speaking American.

King Nebuchadnezzar had a good plan.

▲ Saturate the boys with the Babylonian culture.

▲ Develop loyalty and pride in these future patriots by telling them about the history of this great country.

▲ School them in the Babylonian religion of many gods, mysticism, and superstition.

▲ Make them Babylonians!

The king's plan may have worked with some, but it did not work with Daniel. Daniel's soul was saturated not only with the culture of Israel — its history, its heroes, and its homelands — but Daniel's heart belonged to Israel's God. He would never be a Babylonian, no matter what he read, what he was taught, or what language he was forced to speak. (More on Daniel tomorrow.)

Data Entry

🖉 Look up Daniel 1:4 in your Bible. Why do you think the king wanted boys who were handsome? What difference did it make what they looked like?

_____

_____

_____

_____

_____

🖉 How would it feel to be taken out of your homeland and forced to live in another, adopting foreign traditions and languages?

_____

_____

_____

_____

_____

_____

✏️ King Nebuchadnezzar tried to immerse Daniel in a Babylonian culture. What are some ways the enemy tries to immerse Christians in a worldly culture?

_____

_____

_____

_____

_____

_____

✏️ Work on your passage for memorization.

✏️ What is today's date? _____ Take a few moments to journey to your Prayeramid.

Quotable

"You never know how much you really believe anything until its truth or falsehood become a matter of life and death to you."
C. S. Lewis

Tuesday

Unit Nine • Wisdom Sets a Table

The House Specialty: A Teachable Spirit

Dig Site

Read Proverbs 9:7-9

Artifacts In Situ

⚲ King Nebuchadnezzar's table

Today's Treasure

Instruct a wise man and he will be wiser still; teach a righteous man and he will add to his learning.
Proverbs 9:9

The Israelites followed a strict diet, one that had been set up by the Lord Himself. There were certain foods they weren't allowed to eat, such as pork and lobster, but they did eat lots of fish, fruits, and vegetables. A Babylonian table and the foreign food on it would have immediately caused all kinds of *buzzers* to go off in Daniel's heart. Some Bible scholars believe that King Nebuchadnezzar's table was filled with food that had been offered to Babylonian gods. If Daniel ate it, he would be aligning himself with those who worshiped these false gods. He could not do that. He would not do that.

Daniel came up with an alternate plan which he presented to the steward, the head of the palace staff. God caused this man's heart to show favor to Daniel. Although he initially resisted Daniel's idea for fear he would lose his job, he was persuaded to provide Daniel and his three friends with vegetables and water for a ten-day trial period. He took a chance. He allowed these boys to try something new. He was willing to see what would happen. At the end of the ten days, Daniel and his friends were noticeably healthier and stronger than the other young men. (Don't let the fact escape you here that of the many Hebrews seized by Babylon, only these four were sticking to the strict dietary code on which they had all been raised.)

The steward continued to bring Daniel the vegetables and water he requested. Notice the steward's teachable spirit. He was willing to acknowledge that Daniel's diet was obviously superior to the king's food. He freely admitted that Daniel was right.

You will never get to the point where you know everything. There will always be someone you haven't met, some place you've never been, some food you've never tasted, some tune you've never heard. While Solomon tells us in Ecclesiastes, "There is nothing new under the sun,"[39] this fact remains: Because there is so very much that is and has always been, so much to learn about, we could never know it all. This is especially true when it comes to the Word of God.

In the book of Hebrews, Paul wrote, "For the word of God is living and active. Sharper than any double-edged sword, it penetrates even to dividing soul and spirit, joints and marrow; it judges the thoughts and attitudes of the heart."[40] God's Word is alive! There is no other explanation for how this ancient text can still minister, soothe, heal, and teach. Yet we sometimes take it for granted, especially if we have been brought up in the church and in a Christian home. We might think that we know everything the Bible has to say, but the truth is, we don't. There is always something new to discover, and God will show it to us when we approach His Word with fresh eyes and a teachable spirit.

Having a teachable spirit is simply realizing there is always more to learn. The very best teachers are the ones who continue taking classes themselves. They continue to study, read, and learn. The very best students are the ones who understand the process of learning, which can be summed up in three words: Learning never ends. We can stop being teachable, however, when we refuse to submit to authority and decide we know it all. Even in the middle of our pride, however, God will continue to use people and circumstances to turn us away from what we think we know and turn us toward His Son, Jesus Christ, who is the only source of truth and wisdom.

Data Entry

✎ How do you develop a teachable spirit? What can you do to become more teachable?

_____

_____

_____

✎ I overheard this conversation in the church hallway after Sunday school:
"I am learning so much from you," the young man said to his teacher, who was many years older.
"And I am learning so much from you," the teacher replied.
How could the older, wiser teacher say something like that to his student?

_____

_____

_____

✎ What happens to the person who refuses to learn?

_____

_____

_____

_____

✎ Work on your passage for memorization.

✎ What is today's date? _____ Take a few moments to journey to your Prayeramid.

Quotable

"Not until we have become humble and teachable, standing in awe of God's holiness and sovereignty . . . acknowledging our own littleness, distrusting our own thoughts, and willing to have our minds turned upside down, can divine wisdom become ours." J. I. Packer

Wednesday
Unit Nine • Wisdom Sets a Table

The Main Course: Cleaning Your Plate

My family had a tradition of going out to eat every Friday night. We usually went to the same place, and I usually ordered the same thing. But one Friday night stands out in my memory because something very unusual happened.

We pulled up in the parking lot ready to enjoy a relaxing dinner. As we headed toward the door of this restaurant, however, we noticed a homeless man hanging around. As my family and other diners made their way inside, he was ignored.

We hadn't been in the restaurant long when I noticed the man being seated at a table near us. His waitress was the same one we had. She helped him get situated at his booth and gave him a glass of water. He looked completely out of place in the nice restaurant. His clothes were old and tattered. His long hair desperately needed a good scrubbing. His scraggly beard hung from a thin face that held sad, tired eyes. Carefully, he set his old, shabby hat down on the table next to him and self-consciously attempted to smooth his messy hair. Then he folded his hands respectfully and sat very still as he waited.

Our waitress brought us our meal, and a few minutes after we got our food, he got his. I watched as the waitress brought him a heaping plate of the special that night, spaghetti. I don't

Dig Site

Read Proverbs 9:10-12

Artifacts In Situ

- menu
- dinner plate
- hat

Today's Treasure

The fear of the Lord is the beginning of wisdom, and knowledge of the Holy One is understanding.
Proverbs 9:10

remember everything that was said, but as soon as she set his plate before him, he began to curse. The quiet, homeless man suddenly went off like a bomb. He got really angry. What a scene! The waitress began to cry as the man shouted at her, pointing at his plate and then at her. Everyone in the restaurant was watching. Within seconds, the manager arrived to investigate the uproar. Sobbing, the waitress fled to the kitchen, and the homeless man was escorted back outside. Soon, a busboy cleared the table, and the restaurant got back to normal.

As we were finishing our meal, the waitress returned to our table.

"Do you need anything else?" she asked. She still had tears in her eyes.

Gently, my mom asked her if she was okay. She nodded, and Mom asked, "What happened?"

"Well," she answered, sniffling, "I saw that bum standing outside. I could tell he didn't have anything, and I felt sorry for him." She explained that she got a free meal, whatever the night's special was, when she worked the dinner shift. So she had checked with the manager and asked him if she could give her free meal that night — the spaghetti dinner — to the homeless man.

The manager agreed. The man was invited in and seated at a table. When the waitress brought him his food, he became angry because *he didn't like spaghetti.* Her kindness and compassion were repaid with cursing and complaining. It was not the reaction she had expected. She had made a sacrifice — gone out on a limb — only to be horribly rejected.

Life is all about sitting down at a table where we do not deserve to be. Not one of us deserved to be born. Humanity was invited to this planet by a loving God who wanted to give us His very best, and His kindness and compassion were repaid with cursing and complaining. When we have the healthy, positive, life-giving fear of God that King Solomon mentions, we sit down at Wisdom's table determined to clean our plate, no matter what happens to be served. Our obedience acknowledges God as the One we serve, not the other way around.

As easily as the beggar was invited in that night, he was just as easily escorted back out. He could have walked away full. He could have walked away with a job as a dishwasher or a busboy! The night was full of opportunity! He walked away empty. May that not be said of us when we dine at Wisdom's table. Let's clean our plates, no matter what is served.

Data Entry

🖉 If you had been serving the homeless man that night, what might you have expected the homeless man to do and say when you brought him his meal?

_____
_____
_____
_____
_____

🖉 Are you going to like everything that is *served* to you in this life? How does God want you to react?

_____
_____
_____
_____
_____

🖉 Using what you've learned in this lesson, define the fear of God as though you were explaining it to a first-grader. How would you explain it to a young child?

_____
_____
_____

🖉 Work on your passage for memorization.

🖉 What is today's date? _____ Take a few moments to journey to your Prayeramid.

Quotable

"Godly fear stands apart from earthly fears because it has a positive and life-giving influence. Fear in God is an acknowledgment of who we are and who God is. It is putting ourselves in our proper place in the universe by recognizing the power and wisdom of the Creator." Ed Young, Jr.

Thursday

Unit Nine • Wisdom Sets a Table

The Table Scraps: Leftovers

I couldn't believe it. How could those guys be so mean?

It was my sophomore year of high school, and it was time to vote for our class officers and class favorites. I had heard some boys snickering in the locker room about what a great joke it would be if they could get everyone to vote for Cecil Humphreys[41] for class favorite. Somehow they had succeeded. Cecil's name was announced over the intercom as the sophomore class favorite boy.

Cecil, bless his heart, had absolutely nothing going for him. His family was poor. He came to school dirty and rumpled. He had a learning disability, so he was in a special education class most of the day. He walked with a slump. He was like an unwanted leftover in the refrigerator of high school. Certainly, he had done nothing to deserve getting picked on, but these guys — the good-looking athletes who always sat at the "cool table," the boys with nice homes and clothes — had tagged Cecil as the brunt of their joke. You see, everyone knew who our class favorite girl would be, the lovely and sweet Rachel Edwards. The boys wanted her to have to get her picture made with Cecil. It was so funny to them! And here's the thing: I'm not sure if Cecil was smart

Dig Site

Read Proverbs 9:13-18

Artifacts In Situ

⚲ high school yearbook

Today's Treasure

The woman Folly is loud; she is undisciplined and without knowledge.
Proverbs 9:13

enough to realize that he was the punchline of a very sick joke. Intellectually, he had developmental delays, and he would forever have the mind of a child. What I do know is that those boys knew full well what they had done. What I've always wondered, however, is why they did it.

Christian psychologist Dr. James Dobson says that most teens feel inferior — like they don't measure up — when it comes to three areas: their looks, their intelligence, and their money. Cecil wasn't up to par in any of those three areas. The boys who pulled the prank, however, were quite adequate. But evidently, they didn't feel that way. They felt inferior. They felt so bad about themselves that they took comfort in calling attention to someone who was even worse off.

They felt ugly.
Well, Cecil was uglier.

They felt like they weren't very smart.
But Cecil was an idiot.

They felt deprived because they didn't have all the "stuff" they wanted.
Cecil was as poor as dirt.

If only those guys had known, believed, and accepted what God wanted them to know — about themselves and about Cecil, too. Will you believe God's Word?

God says that you are fearfully and wonderfully made, whether or not you make the team (Psalm 139:14).

God says that you are chosen, holy and dearly loved, whether or not you have the approval of people (Colossians 3:12).

God says that you are His child, and you look like your Father, even with your teenage skin and awkward body (I John 3:1,2).

God says that you are accepted because of your faith in Jesus Christ, whether or not you feel accepted by other people (Galatians 2:16).

God says that you are wealthy because He will meet all your needs, according to His glorious riches in Christ (Philippians 4:19).

In hindsight, I suspect each of those young men wanted to be class favorite. Rather than be nominated and lose the class vote, they chose to control the election. Then they wouldn't have to deal with rejection or loss if they didn't get the nod. Instead, it was all a joke, and they could go home laughing, their self-esteem "intact."

What about Cecil?

Cecil, child-like Cecil, arrived on picture day in an ill-fitting three-piece suit, and he got his picture made with Rachel Edwards. But he didn't smile.

Data Entry

🖉 Matthew 25:31-45 are the words of Christ as He outlined the distinction that will be made, when He comes again, between the those who served God and those who didn't. Copy the words of the King in verse 40 here.

_____

_____

_____

🖉 Do you think the actions of the boys would have been different if they had stopped to recognize that Cecil was made in Christ's image, and whatever they did to him, they were doing to Christ Jesus?

_____

_____

_____

🖉 What if just one of those boys had said, "I don't think it would be right to do that to Cecil"? What if just one of those boys had tried to be his friend?

_____

_____

_____

_____

✏ How will you live your life now that you know what God says about you and about others?

_____

_____

_____

_____

✏ Bible teacher Beth Moore once encouraged a group of mission workers to recite this "pledge of faith" (below), which she uses daily.42 As you conclude your study of the first nine chapters of Proverbs, you may want to make this part of your morning routine. Copy it on a note card to post on your mirror or beside your bed.

My Pledge of Faith
God is who He says He is.
God can do what He says He can do.
I am who God says I am.
I can do all things through Christ.
God's Word is alive and active in me.

✏ Work on your passage for memorization.

✏ What is today's date? _____ Take a few moments to journey to your Prayeramid.

Quotable

"The reason conformity is so dangerous is that it can cause you to do things that you know are wrong. This is what happens when you don't have the courage to be different from your friends." Dr. James Dobson

Friday

Unit Nine • Wisdom Sets a Table

Lab Work: Artifacts and Heartifacts

➪ Read back through Proverbs 9 and your data entries for this week.

➪ Complete any unanswered questions from this week's lessons.

➪ What will last from your study of Proverbs 9? List this week's Artifacts and Heartifacts below.

Artifacts	**Heartifacts**
_____	_____
_____	_____
_____	_____
_____	_____

➪ Do some soul-searching about what God is teaching you. Record your thoughts below.

_____

_____

_____

_____

_____

➪ Work on your Scripture memory passage. You can do it!

➪ Take a few moments to journey to your Prayeramid.

➪ Don't forget this week's EXTRA! Finish reading the book of Ecclesiastes.

About Quotables

Each lesson includes a quote from a remarkable Christian. You probably recognized some of the names, but others may have been new to you. Below are brief biographies of the wise men behind each Quotable.

Neil T. Anderson is the president emeritus of Freedom in Christ Ministries and a much sought-after speaker on Christ-centered living. Besides the best-selling books *The Bondage Breaker®*, *Victory over the Darkness*, and *Daily in Christ,* he has also coauthored many books, including *Getting Anger Under Control* and *Breaking the Bondage of Legalism.*

Dietrich Bonhoeffer died at the age of 39 at Flossenburg concentration camp. He was a German religious leader (a Lutheran pastor and theologian) and participated in the resistance movement against Nazism. His efforts to help a group of Jews escape to Switzerland led to his first arrest. His religious writings give us a keen look into that period of history and Bonhoeffer's deep faith in Christ as he lived through it.

The late **Larry Burkett** was the founder and president of Christian Financial Concepts, Inc., a ministry dedicated to teaching God's principles for financial management. During his life he wrote over 70 books, including the recently updated classic, *Business by the Book: The Complete Guide of Biblical Principles for the Workplace.*

John Calvin was an important French Christian theologian during the Protestant reformation. He is the founder of the system of Christian theology that bears his name: Calvinism.

S. Truett Cathy is the founder and chairman of Chick-Fil-A®, a national chain of quick service chicken restaurants; founder of WinShape Centre Foundation®, a charitable organization for youth; and author of *Eat Mor Chikin: Inspire More People.*

Jesus Christ is the Son of God, the source of the Christian religion, and the Savior of the world. Conceived miraculously by His mother, Mary, through the Holy Spirit, He grew to be received as a great teacher by disciples and common people alike. He preached the redeeming love of God for every person. He was seized by the Romans but turned over to and crucified by Jewish authorities. Rising again on the third day, Christ offers forgiveness of sin and eternal life in Heaven to all who believe He is God's promised Messiah and surrender to His Lordship.

Charles "Chuck" Colson is a popular and widely-known author, speaker, and radio commentator. A former presidential aide to Richard Nixon and founder of the international ministry Prison Fellowship, he has written several books, including *Born Again, Loving God,* and *Kingdoms in Conflict.*

Clay Crosse is a husband, father, and three-time Dove Award-winning singer who has spent more than a decade recording and performing world-wide. He has nine number one singles. Married since 1990, Clay and his wife Renee began HolyHomes ministries in 2002, which challenges Christian families to live godly lives. They have written a book together, *I Surrender All: Rebuilding a Marriage Broken by Pornography.* Visit www.claycrosse.com.

Dr. Don Colbert, M.D. is a board-certified family practitioner. He is the author of several best-selling books, including *What Would Jesus Eat?* Dr. Colbert helps people develop strategies for managing the stresses of life in ways that benefit them physically, emotionally, and spiritually.

King David was the son of Jesse. Growing up as a shepherd boy, he was anointed by the prophet Samuel as Israel's future king. He is known in Scripture as a man after God's own heart. Many of his writings are featured in the book of Psalms. He was a giant-slayer, worship leader, friend, husband, father, and king.

Mark Dewey is married to Monique and they have nine children in their home, bringing them great joy. Mark has thirteen years of experience in professional baseball, pitching at the major and minor league levels (San Francisco Giants, New York Mets, and Pittsburgh Pirates) and coaching for two years for the Kingsport Mets. He is a pastor of Christ the King Church in Michigan and oversees the ministry of Athletes Abroad for Christ (AAFC). Visit www.athletesabroadforchrist.com.

Dr. James Dobson is a licensed psychologist and the president of Focus on the Family Ministries. In addition, he is heard regularly on more than 4,000 radio stations worldwide. He has written numerous books and is perhaps the contemporary Christian family's most ardent supporter, beloved encourager, and sought-after counselor.

The late **Theodore Epp**, a graduate of Southwestern Theological Seminary, Ft. Worth, Texas, was the founding director of the *Back to the Bible* broadcast. The ministry currently has 13 overseas offices and produces 9 different programs in native languages.

Billy Graham is a world-renowned author, preacher, and evangelist. He has delivered the Gospel to more people face-to-face than anyone in history, ministering on all seven continents. Some have called him, "America's pastor." Read Rev. Graham's fascinating memoirs in his autobiography, *Just as I Am*.

A. C. Green currently owns the NBA Iron Man title, having played in 1,192 straight games. He is known not only for his pro-basketball career, but also for the fact that he kept his virginity until he married in 2002, at the age of 38. Today A.C. is a youth mentor, author, speaker, and successful businessman who is committed to sexual abstinence education. Visit www.acgreen.com.

Joshua Harris is senior pastor of Covenant Life Church outside Washington, D.C., where he lives with his wife Shannon and their children. While in his early twenties, this homeschool graduate started a revolution with the publication of his book, *I Kissed Dating Good-Bye*. Check out his website, www.joshharris.com.

Vance Havner was a great revival evangelist of the 20th Century. He is one of the most quoted preachers of all time. He was known for frank, straightforward sermons that never sugarcoated the reality of sin or the redemption of the Savior.

Doug Herman is an international speaker and author who has spent over 20 years in youth and family work. Having lost a wife and daughter to AIDS, Doug has emerged from this tragedy strong and true. Currently, Doug speaks to over 250,000 teens and adults yearly about character development, sexual abstinence, and spiritual passion. Learn more about Doug at www.dougherman.com.

Lamont Hiebert is a vocalist and songwriter for the band *Ten Shekel Shirt*. He wrote his first song, "Sing for Joy," when he was 21 years old. *Ten Shekel Shirt* (INO/EPIC Records) merges melodic college rock with Brit pop/rock. Their acoustic driven 2001 debut album, "Much," sold 130,000 units and featured the #1 hit "Ocean." Visit www.tenshekelshirt.com.

Jerry B. Jenkins, former vice president for publishing and currently writer-at-large for the Moody Bible Institute of Chicago, is the author of more than 150 books, including the best-selling *Left Behind* series. Learn more at his website, www.jerryjenkins.com.

Meb Keflezighi became the first American man since 1976 to win an Olympic medal in the men's marathon, taking the silver at Panathenaiko Stadium at the 2004 Olympic Games in Athens.

C. S. Lewis was one of the intellectual giants of the twentieth century and some believe the most influential Christian writer of his day. His writings, including *The Chronicles of Narnia,* continue to be widely read today.

Eric Liddell was an Olympian runner who publicly professed to his faith in Christ. His time in the 100-meter race stood as England's best for thirty-five years. However, during the Paris Olympics in the summer of 1924, the qualifying race for the 100-meter was to be held on a Sunday. Liddell refused to run on what he considered to be a sacred day. Three days later, he took part in the 400-meter race. No one expected him to win, but he did. He won the gold and set a world record. The movie, "Chariots of Fire," chronicles his life.

Chief Justice Roy Moore is also known as "The Ten Commandments Judge." He has gained national recognition for his courageous defense of the Ten Commandments in the face of career-threatening opposition. He is the author of several books, including *So Help Me God: The Ten Commandments, Judicial Tyranny, and the Battle for Religious Freedom.*

Blaise Pascal was a French mathematician, physicist, and religious philosopher. He suffered from many illnesses throughout his life, living most of his adult life in great pain. He pledged his life to Christianity and was able to find harmony between his scientific training and his spiritual beliefs.

J. I. Packer is Sangwoo Youtong Chee Professor of Theology at Regent College in Vancouver and the author of many books, including the contemporary classic, *Knowing God*.

Dennis Rainey is the executive director and the co-founder of FamilyLife (a division of Campus Crusade for Christ) and the daily host of the nationally syndicated radio program "FamilyLife Today." Visit www.familylife.com.

Dave Ramsey is a personal money management expert, a popular national radio personality, and the best-selling author of *Financial Peace* and *The Total Money Makeover*. Dave devotes himself full-time to helping ordinary people understand the forces behind their financial distress and how to set things right financially, emotionally, and spiritually. Visit www.daveramsey.com.

Stephen S. Sawyer is internationally known for his *Art for God* series. The reproductions can be found in over 100 countries and in every state of the union. His art has been featured on the front page of the New York Times, appeared in the Wall Street Journal, and been featured in virtually every major city in America. He has promoted the life and teachings of Jesus with his art in over 400 newspapers and hundreds of radio stations here and abroad. Stephen's need to visually express the profound nature of living faith is the driving momentum and influence behind his work. Visit www.art4god.com.

Rick Warren is the founding pastor of Saddleback Church in Lake Forest, California. He and his wife, Kay, began the church in their home in January 1980, with one family. Today, Saddleback is one of America's largest and best-known churches. Rick is the author of the best-selling book, *The Purpose-Driven Life*.

Warren Wiersbe (Th. B., Northern Baptist Seminary) is one of the evangelical world's most respected Bible teachers. His speaking, writing, and radio ministries have clearly and consistently proclaimed the gospel of Jesus Christ around the world for more than thirty years.

Ed Young, Jr. is the Senior Pastor of Fellowship Church in Grapevine, Texas. Ed also hosts *Creative Connection,* a nationally syndicated weekday radio program and weekly television program on TBN and Daystar. He is the author of several popular books including *High Definition Living* and *The Creative Marriage*.

Appendix A

Zig Ziglar walked away from a record-setting sales career to help other people become more successful in their personal and professional lives. His name is synonymous with confidence, motivation, and success. A master at motivational speaking, Zig has that rare ability to make audiences comfortable and relaxed, yet completely attentive. As an author, he has written nine books, including the perennial best-seller, *See You At The Top,* with over two million copies in print.

Scripturistics!
Deciphering the Code

Studying God's Word will pave the way for you to understand your culture and the challenging times in which you live. Sometimes young people think of the Bible as a difficult book to read, but with the many contemporary English versions that are currently available, that is simply not true. I encourage you to find a Bible version that you understand and enjoy reading.

For hundreds of years, generations of scholars, theologians, linguists, and priests have worked diligently to translate God's Word into common languages for common man. Many gave their lives in order for the Holy Scripture to be made available to the common man. So read it! Dig deep into the Word of God! It will give you the keys you need for unlocking the mysteries of life.

Why Memorize Scripture?

Part of becoming the man God wants you to be includes memorizing His Word. Memorizing Scripture will give you a foundation on which to build your Christian life. It has been proven to increase confidence, relieve worries, and greatly improve one's thought life.

Why should you memorize Scripture? Explaining the necessity of memorizing Scripture is much like explaining the reason for eating. We must feed our bodies for nourishment, protection against disease, cleansing, and strength, and we do this out of obedience to God.

Nourishment

Why do you feed your body? Food fuels your body and keeps it functioning. Without food, you would lack the energy you need for living. But you're not just a body. Your body houses your spirit. How do you feed it?

Jesus said, "It takes more than bread to stay alive. It takes a steady stream of words from God's mouth."[43] He was talking about your spirit's need for nourishment. Your spirit is fed by God's Word.

Unearthing the Treasures of Solomon's Proverbs

Protection against disease

There is an old saying that goes, "My food is my medicine. My medicine is my food." Obviously, if you want your body to operate properly, you must eat the right foods. Part of your body's capacity to function lies in its ability to produce antibodies that fight and protect against disease. With the proper nutrients (food), your body can perform this task with ease.

Numbers of studies have been conducted that show how some foods can help fight and even prevent cancer. Natural herbs and spices are used today to treat medical ailments. Centuries ago, the Native American tribes were known for mixing up all kinds of medicines to treat various illnesses, and today's medical doctors are going back to nature to find remedies for the sick.

Your spirit is diseased and sick because of sin. Sin is sickness that affects everyone. God's Word is a healing balm to soothe the sores left by sin. His Word is a medicine that can take away your sin — providing total healing — through Jesus Christ.

Cleansing

Did you know that certain foods can clean your body on the inside? For example, drinking lots of water each day washes out your digestive system. It cleanses your body of impurities.

The Bible says that Jesus washes the Church with the water of the Word.[44] Knowing God's Word thoroughly can wash the enemy's lies right off your spirit. The enemy, Satan, likes to throw dirt on God's children. "You can't do anything right!" he whispers, like a snake.

However, when you know God's Word, those filthy lies cannot stain you. You can wipe them off by speaking the Truth. "I can do everything through Him who gives me strength!"[45]

To help others

If you didn't eat anything, you would not be able to help anyone. You would become so weak that you would be powerless to do anything. You would be unable to help around the house. You could not do anything to assist your siblings, parents, or grandparents. In fact, other people would be called in to help you. With proper nutrition, your body is strong. You can work. You can serve. You can be a blessing to those who need you.

In the same way, when you know God's Word, you are strong enough to help other people. You can provide them with godly counsel. You can give good advice. You can help them find their way through problems.

Your Father says so

Your parents want you to eat because they know the benefits of good health. They know the role that good foods play in growing strong muscles and bones, and so do you.

Your Heavenly Father, God, wants you to memorize His Word. He wants you to "eat" it — take it in until it becomes a part of you. God told Joshua, "Ponder and meditate on it [Scripture] day and night, making sure you practice everything written in it. Then you'll get where you're going; then you'll succeed."[46]

God's Word is:

>A Revelation

>>A Signpost

>>>A Life-Map...................

>>>>The Direction to Successful Living

God's Word warns us of danger and directs us to hidden treasure. Otherwise how will we find our way?[47]

Tips for Memorizing Scripture

Memorize one verse at a time.

We are memorizing large blocks of Scripture in this Bible study. Let's go at them one verse at a time.

Memorize phrase by phrase.

Once you copy down your verse, see if you can break it up into phrases. Underline, use different colored pens or markers, and break up the verse.

Buddy Up.
Ask a parent, sibling, or friend to memorize the verse with you. Work on the verse together. Hold each other accountable!

Write the verse.
Write out the Scripture in your own handwriting on a 3x5 note card, a sticky note, or regular paper. Studies have shown that writing things down helps you remember them.

Read the verse.
▲ Listen to yourself as you read the verse aloud several times each day.
▲ Laminate the passage or cover it with clear Contact™ paper and post it in the shower. "Sing" the Scripture to a tune you make up!

Listen to the verse.
▲ Record yourself reading the verse aloud.
▲ Make an audio tape of different people reading the verse aloud. Ask family members, your pastor and other teachers at church, and your friends to read the verse. Ask them to read the verse slowly, phrase by phrase, so you will have time to repeat after them.
▲ Listen to the tape. Play the tape for your siblings and see if they can guess to whom each voice belongs.

Think about the verse.
▲ Post the verse beside your bed. Think about the verse as you drift off to sleep at night.
▲ Put the verse beside your bathroom mirror. Think about what the verse means as you brush your teeth.
▲ Write the verse on a sticky note and put it on the front of one of your school folders. Interchange with the next verse when you have learned the first one.

Do the verse.
Researchers have found that an active body promotes an active mind. Get your body moving and your blood pumping, and it will rev up your brain cells!

▲ Make up motions to go along with the verse.

▲ Bounce or dribble a ball while you memorize.

▲ Take a walk with your verse cards in hand.

▲ Try jumping rope while you work on your Scripture.

Create a rewards program.

With your parents' approval, come up with a rewards system for your hard work. Draw up a contract and agree that you will only receive the reward when the verse is completely memorized, word for word. (Please note: Memorizing Scripture is a reward in and of itself. It is a lasting treasure. However, I don't see anything wrong with rewarding young people for learning the disciplines of hard work and commitment.)

Suggested Scripture Memory Passages

Deuteronomy 30:15-20	Proverbs 3:1-8	2 Timothy 2:22-26
1 Samuel 12:20-25	John 15:9-12	James 1:19-25
Psalm 1	Ephesians 4:25-31	James 2:14-18
Psalm 23	Philippians 2:5-11	
Psalm 24	Philippians 4:10-13	

Prayeramids

Just like a pyramid has four sides, prayer has four parts:

▲ Praising God for who He is,
▲ Repenting (asking forgiveness) for your sins,
▲ Thanking God for the blessings He gives, and
▲ Requesting God's provision, strength, and mercy for yourself and others.

Prayer can happen anytime, anywhere. You will find prayer amid sickness, prayer amid joy, prayer amid confusion, and prayer amid conflict. As you conclude your time of Bible study each day, use these "prayeramids" as a guide for your own prayers to God. Each prayer is based on a key verse from one of the thirty-one chapters in Proverbs. Coordinate the prayers to the day's date. For example, if today was September 12, you would read the 12th prayer. Tomorrow, you would read the 13th prayer. Pray through these 31 prayers every month. Use these prayers as a springboard to deeper conversations with God.

1 **Father,** I praise You. You alone are worthy of my praise. Forgive me for the times that I don't put You first in my life. Thank You for creating me and giving me breath. Help me to give You my reverence and worship. May I fear You, Lord, and serve Christ alone.
The fear of the Lord is the beginning of knowledge; fools despise wisdom and discipline. Proverbs 1:7

2 **Father,** I worship You today. You are all powerful. Your angels surround me, guarding me. Please forgive me when I don't trust You to protect me. Thank You for being my Shield and my Defense. Father, please keep me away from wrong people, wrong places, and dangerous situations.
. . . so that He may guard the paths of justice and protect the way of His loyal followers. Proverbs 2:8

3 **Father,** You are my eternal hope. My heart is Yours. I'm sorry for the times I put myself first instead of You first. I understand that I am to have no other gods before You. Please help me think of You first and acknowledge Your Lordship in everything I do and say.
Trust in the Lord with all your heart and do not rely on your own understanding; think about Him in all your ways, and He will guide you on the right paths. Proverbs 3:5,6

4 **Father,** You are the Wonderful Counselor. You are Wisdom and Truth. I admit I make foolish choices sometimes. Please forgive me, Lord. As I get older, my decisions become more important. Please give me the wisdom of Christ, and teach me to guard my heart.
Guard your heart above all else, for it is the source of life. Proverbs 4:23

5 **Father,** You are holy, good, and perfect. I'm not like You, Lord, but I want to be. Please help me to stay pure in my thoughts, my words, and my actions. Help me to guard my eyes and my heart. Give me the strength to wait for my wife and to save my body for her alone.
Though the lips of the forbidden woman drip honey and her words are smoother than oil, in the end she's as bitter as wormwood and as sharp as a double-edged sword. Proverbs 5:3,4

6 **Father,** You are the Lord of the harvest. You planned for work to be part of life. I'm sorry for having a bad attitude about my chores and schoolwork sometimes. Help me to be diligent in my work. Please develop my gifts and skills so that I can serve You in the work You call me to do.
Go to the ant, you slacker! Observe its ways and become wise! Proverbs 6:6

7 **Father,** You are all-knowing. You hold the future in Your hands. I don't know if You plan for me to get married one day, but if You do, that means that my wife is out there somewhere. Protect her purity, God. Give her the strength to wait for me.

For she has brought many down to death; her victims are countless. Her house is the road to Sheol, descending to the chambers of death. Proverbs 7:26, 27

8 **Father,** Thank You for choosing me. Thank You for choosing to send a Redeemer, Jesus, to save me. Lord, You always make wise choices. Please teach me how to make good decisions. I want to choose the very best — the things that will lead me closer to You. Help me in choosing the right direction for my life.

Accept my instruction instead of silver, and knowledge rather than pure gold, for wisdom is better than precious stones, and nothing desirable can compare with it. Proverbs 8:10,11

9 **Father,** You know everything. Sometimes I don't care one bit about school, Lord. I don't feel like reading or writing or doing my math. Please instill in me a love of learning. Help me to understand that everything I'm learning is helping me to prepare for the life You have planned for me.

Instruct a wise man, and he will be wiser still, teach a righteous man, and he will learn more. Proverbs 9:9

10 **Father,** It's amazing to think that Jesus never said a wrong thing. I say wrong things every single day. I want my mouth to obey You, Lord. Please help me to say only things that are kind. Help me to build others up and not criticize and insult people, especially my family.

The mouth of the righteous is a fountain of life, but the mouth of the wicked conceals violence. Proverbs 10:11

11 **Father,** You gave up everything for me, even Your own Son. I can be really stingy sometimes, Lord. Help me to be a giving person. Help me to share — not just my things, but also my time, my space, and my attention.
One man gives freely, yet gains even more; another withholds unduly, but comes to poverty. Proverbs 11:24

12 **Father,** You have provided standards for living in the Ten Commandments. The Bible is Your instruction book. I don't know why, but I still have trouble sometimes knowing exactly what I should do in certain situations. I need godly counselors in my life, Lord. And I need You to help me to listen to them.
The way of a fool seems right to him, but a wise man listens to advice. Proverbs 12:15

13 **Father,** You give me everything I need. You are always faithful to me. So Lord, I'm asking: I need some good friends. Please lead me to people who will help me in my Christian walk. Show me other kids my age who want to serve You; lead me to people who are really living out their faith. Please give me godly friends, and help me to be one, too.
He who walks with the wise grows wise, but a companion of fools suffers harm. Proverbs 13:20

14 **Father,** You can see right through me. You know my innermost thoughts. I pray that You will give me the wisdom of a discerning spirit regarding people, places, and circumstances. Even if it looks good on the outside, it may not be good for me. Help me know when I am with someone who will bring trouble to my life or when I am somewhere You don't want me to be.
There is a way that seems right to a man, but in the end it leads to death. Proverbs 14:12

15 **Father,** According to You, I am fearfully and wonderfully made. I sure don't feel that way, Lord. Sometimes I feel like my body is out of control. Help me to take care of my body by eating right, exercising everyday, and keeping a smile on my face. Help me to remember my body is Your temple.
A cheerful look brings joy to the heart, and good news gives health to the bones. Proverbs 15:30

▲

16 **Father,** Why do I act this way? I don't mean to talk back, and I don't mean to be rude to my family. I don't know what comes over me, Lord. At the time, the things I say and do seem right. Then I realize that I shouldn't have, and I wish I hadn't. Please give me greater self-control.
Better a patient man than a warrior, a man who controls his temper than one who takes a city. Proverbs 16:32

▲

17 **Father,** Without Your forgiveness, I would be lost. Father, forgive me when I am slow to forgive others — when I hold on to hurts. I end up getting more hurt that way. Please help me to live a life of ongoing forgiveness, not necessarily because I feel like it, but because forgiveness is what You ask me to do.
He who covers over an offense promotes love, but whoever repeats the matter separates close friends. Proverbs 17:9

▲

18 **Father,** You are my best friend. You loved me enough to die for me. Your Word says that a friend loves all the time. I want to learn to be a good friend. Please help me to understand what that means. Forgive me for my selfishness and for not putting others first. Help me to be patient and kind and fun to be around. Help me to be the kind of friend others are looking for.
A man of many companions may come to ruin, but there is a friend who sticks closer than a brother. Proverbs 18:24

19 **Father,** Even Jesus had to obey His mom and dad. I'm sure that He did it much more cheerfully than I do at times. It is so hard sometimes! They have opinions about everything, Lord. I want to please them, but they sure do ask a lot from me! Please help me to mind my parents, to love them, and to honor them with my respectful submission.
He who obeys instructions guards his life, but he who is contemptuous of his ways will die. Proverbs 19:16

▲

20 **Father,** Drugs and alcohol are a trap. They look like a party, but they are a funeral. Instead of living, people just start dying when they get involved with drugs. I don't want to miss out on a job, a home, and a family. I pray that I will never fall for that trap. Please, Lord, guard my life from the destruction of addictions.
Wine is a mocker and beer a brawler; whoever is led astray by them is not wise. Proverbs 20:1

▲

21 **Father,** I praise You, O Lord. You alone are worthy. God, I'm sorry. Today I just got tired of being good. I got tired of trying. Now I'm miserable. Help me to run this race called life with a steadfast determination to make it to the finish line. Help me to keep putting one foot in front of the other, whether I feel like it or not. Keep me in hot pursuit of righteousness and love.
He who pursues righteousness and love finds life, prosperity, and honor. Proverbs 21:21

▲

22 **Father,** Yours is the Name above all Names. I want to be known for having a good name, too, Lord. In many ways, it is important what others think about me. I want to be known for being a Christian, Lord. That sounds pretty simple, but I don't think it's going to be easy. Guard my reputation, Lord. May my actions only bring you glory, never shame.
A good name is more desirable than great riches; to be esteemed is better than silver or gold. Proverbs 22:22

Unearthing the Treasures of Solomon's Proverbs

23   **Father,** You are so great! Let me thank You today for everything I can think of. Maybe that will help me quit wanting so much more. I keep asking Mom and Dad for stuff; it's like I'm out of control! Teach me to be content with what You provide.
Do not wear yourself out to get rich; have the wisdom to show restraint.
Proverbs 23:4

▲

24   **Father,** I'm so glad that You created families. I wonder what mine will be like. I know that no matter what, You have a good plan for my life. Please show me the path I am to take, and help me to follow every step as You lead me. Whether I am single or married, childless or the head of a house full of kids, please bless my future home.
By wisdom a house is built, and through understanding it is established; through knowledge its rooms are filled with rare and beautiful treasures.
Proverbs 24:3,4

▲

25   **Father,** The more I learn about You, Lord, the more it seems You tell me to do the opposite of what I want to do! Love my enemies? Pray for the people who mistreat me? It's really hard to treat other people the way that You would treat them. May I live by the Golden Rule, Lord, because the truth is, that's the way I want others to treat me: with grace, understanding, and love.
If your enemy is hungry, give him food to eat; if he is thirsty, give him water to drink. In doing this, you will heap burning coals on his head, and the Lord will reward you. Proverbs 25:21,22

▲

26   **Father,** I can't do anything without You, Lord. And yet I find myself many times thinking that I can. I can be nice. I can be respectful. I can have self-control. But I can't. Not without Your help. I don't want to be full of myself, Lord. I want to be full of You. Teach me true humility, Lord, and may I not be prideful.
Do you see a man wise in his own eyes? There is more hope for a fool than for him. Proverbs 26:12

27 **Father,** I want my friends and everyone that I meet to know that I am a Christian. I want them to see Jesus all over me. I don't just want Him in my heart, Lord. I want Him in my smile, my laughter, my compassion, and my attitude. May my heart reflect the One who lives there, Jesus Christ. And may He shine through my thoughts, my words, and my deeds.
As water reflects a face, so a man's heart reflects the man. Proverbs 27:19

28 **Father,** Please bring to my mind now the sins that I may have pushed toward the back of my brain. Help me to recall the sins that I haven't asked forgiveness for. And Lord, even if it might be terribly difficult, please show me if there is anyone whose forgiveness I need to ask. Have I hurt someone and not apologized? On the flip side, is there someone with whom I am upset, someone I need to forgive? It doesn't matter if that person has asked my forgiveness. I need to forgive simply to be right with You. Search my heart — reveal my foolish ways.
He who conceals his sins does not prosper, but whoever confesses and renounces them finds mercy. Proverbs 28:13

29 **Father,** Sometimes I am afraid of what people will think about me. I try too hard to be who I think others are expecting me to be. That's not right. You made me to be Your own special treasure. You are the One Who loves me most. You created my personality and the way I am. Help me to be myself. I want to be a God-pleaser, not a people-pleaser.
Fear of man will prove to be a snare, but whoever trusts in the Lord is kept safe. Proverbs 29:25

30 **Father,** Sometimes I just don't feel like picking up my Bible. I'm sorry, Lord. Would You please make it be like candy to me? Make it something I just can't resist! Help me to love it more, and lead me to study it with my whole heart. I know there are great truths and riches to be found in the Bible. May I desire the wonders found only in Your Word.
Every word of God is flawless; He is a shield to those who take refuge in Him. Proverbs 30:5

31 **Father,** I want to be able to provide godly counsel and words of righteous wisdom to my friends when they're in trouble. I want to help people who are in need. I want other people to know that Jesus really is the only way to God. And Lord, I want to share your love by loving and serving others. Use me as a defender and a protector of people, and give me boldness to live an authentic Christian life. Make me the man You want me to be.
Speak up, judge righteously, and defend the cause of the oppressed and needy. Proverbs 31:30

About the Author

Rebecca Ingram Powell is a pastor's wife, homeschooling mother of three, and a nationally known author and speaker. She received a Bachelor of Arts degree in English with a minor in Speech Communications, graduating magna cum laude with Distinction of University Honors from Middle Tennessee State University. Rebecca and her husband Rich were college sweethearts and today live in a suburb of Nashville, Tennessee, with their three children, Danya, David, and Derek. The Powells are members of Madison First Baptist Church where Rich serves as Minister of Missions.

Other Books by Rebecca:

Wise Up! Experience the Power of Proverbs (for girls)

Baby Boot Camp: Basic Training for the First Six Weeks of Motherhood (for new moms)

Speaking Engagements

For information on booking Rebecca for speaking engagements, please visit www.rebeccapowell.com.

End Notes

1. Matthew 7:13-14 (NLT)
2. John 18:1-11
3. 1 Peter 1:15-16 (Msg)
4. This video is available from Nantucket Publishing. Web: www.unshackled.com, Toll-free: 1.800.430.7719, Email: Nantucket@yahoo.com.
5. Isaiah 28:13
6. Proverbs 1:7 (Msg)
7. Harold Morris, *Twice Pardoned: An Ex-Con Talks to Parents and Teens* (Pomora, Calif.: Focus on the Family Publishing, 1986), 1.
8. 1 Corinthians 15:33 (GOD'S WORD)
9. Galatians 6:8 (Msg)
10. Sister Helen Mrosla's article was later reprinted in *Reader's Digest* and ultimately found a home on the Internet. It has been adapted for *Dig Deep*. 27 Dec. 2005 <http://www.truthorfiction.com/rumors/m/markeklund.htm>.
11. © 1985 Word Music (a division of Word, Inc.) and Stonehillian Music (ASCAP).
12. Anderson, Neil. "Spiritual Discernment." The Faithful Hope Reading Room. 27 Dec. 2005 <http://www.faithfulhope.com/readingroom/item.cfm?doc_id=7998>.
13. Gay, Nancy. "Statement from Mark Dewey." San Francisco Chronicle, 5 Aug. 1996, 27 Dec. 2005 <http://www.sfgate.com/cgi-bin/article.cgi?f=/c/a/1996/08/05/SP43218.DTL&hw= Nancy+Gay&sn=012&sc=331>.
14. Mike Griffin's written narrative was excerpted from *A Woman's Secret to a Balanced Life* (Harvest House, 2004) by Lysa TerKeurst and Sharon Jaynes.
15. Naber, John. John Naber's Simple Advice . . . 'No Deposit, No Return.' 21 Apr. 2004, 27 Dec. 2005 <http://www.olympic-usa.org/132_18776.htm>.
16. Matthew 7:13 (Msg)
17. 2 Samuel 24:24b
18. Hebrews 11:1
19. Matthew 5:27-28
20. Stenzel, Pam. Sex has Price Tag. Adapted for *Dig Deep*. 27 Dec. 2005 <http://www.prolife.com/stenzel.htm>. Pam has a dynamic video of her eye-opening *Sex Has A Price Tag* presentation. Her message is compelling and unforgettable. To order, send a suggested donation of $25.00 payable to Pro-Life America to: Pro-Life America, Pam Stenzel Video Dept, 1840 S. Elena Ave., # 103, Redondo Beach, CA 90277.
21. (Msg)
22. Matthew 12:36 (Msg)

23 Merriam-Webster Online Dictionary. <http://www.merriamwebster.com>.

24 (TEV)

25 (GOD'S WORD)

26 (BBE)

27 Used with permission from Lisa Whelchel.

28 James 1:13-14

29 I Peter 5:8

30 Morris, Marilyn. "He Said, She Said." <u>Tips for Encouraging Sexual Abstinence</u>. January, 2004: 1-2.

31 Doug is paraphrasing Luke 7:23.

32 (Msg)

33 Mark 1:16-18

34 Matthew 26:31a (NLT)

35 Matthew 26:33 (NLT)

36 Matthew 26:34 (NLT)

37 Luke 22:59b-61a

38 Daniel 1:4 (NLT)

39 Ecc. 1:9

40 Hebrews 4:12

41 Names in this lesson have been changed.

42 Roten, Manda. "Beth Moore: Pour out your life & believe God for the impossible." <u>BP News</u>, 30 Oct. 2003, 27 Dec. 2005 <http://www.bpnews.net/bpnews.asp?ID=16966>.

43 Matthew 4:4 (Msg)

44 Ephesians 5:26

45 Philippians 4:13

46 Joshua 1:8b (Msg)

47 Psalm 19:11 (Msg)

To order additional copies of

DIG DEEP

Unearthing the Treasures of Solomon's Proverbs

Please visit www.rebeccapowell.com

Or have your credit card ready and call:
Pleasant Word
1-877-421-READ (7323)

Printed in the United States
98661LV00002B/127-146/A